THE PATTERN OF NEW TESTAMENT TRUTH

The Pattern
of
New Testament Truth

by

George Eldon Ladd

Professor of New Testament Exegesis and Theology
Fuller Theological Seminary

WILLIAM B. EERDMANS PUBLISHING COMPANY

Grand Rapids, Michigan

Foreword

The invitation to deliver the Nils W. Lund Memorial Lectures at North Park Seminary, Chicago, Illinois, on November 15 and 16, 1966, provided me with the incentive to work out an idea which long ago occurred to me which illustrates the elements of unity and diversity in New Testament theology. The thesis could be expanded to include other New Testament writings, particularly Hebrews and Revelation. But since the Synoptics, John, and Paul represent the most important strands of New Testament thought, the discussion may be limited to them without impairing the central thesis.

The author would express thanks to Dean Donald C. Frisk, and to the faculty and students of North Park Seminary for their cordial reception and hearty interaction with the lectures, which are here published practically as they were delivered.

GEORGE ELDON LADD

Pasadena, California

Table of Contents

Chapter One

The Background of the Pattern:
Greek or Hebrew?

Introduction

The student of biblical thought must concern himself with interests far broader than the teaching of given portions of the Bible. He has only begun his task when he has grasped the meaning of the Kingdom of God, the Son of Man, eternal life, justification, the work of the Holy Spirit, and the like. His work is not even done when he succeeds in understanding comprehensively the message of Jesus, the kerygma of the primitive church, the theology of Paul and John. The analytic fashion of an earlier generation is now passé. The modern biblical theologian can no longer be satisfied to conclude his work with the reconstruction of a number of separate, independent theologies or *Lehrbegriffe*.[1]

Fifty years ago, the effort to find a basic unity in New Testament theology risked the haughty disdain of so-called scientific scholars, who saw this effort as an apologetic device for an orthodox view of the Bible. However, fashions even in scholarship change, and one of the present emphases in New Testament studies, at least in the English-speaking world, was founded by C. H. Dodd who, in his inaugural lecture at Cambridge University in 1935, called for a new recognition of the unity of New Testament thought in place of the severe analysis that had prevailed throughout the preceding century. The exclusive

[1] See the New Testament theologies of B. Weiss, W. Beyschlag, H. J. Holtzmann, P. Feine, G. B. Stevens.

dominance of the analytic approach had "led to a piecemeal treatment of early Christian thought, which in the end made it more difficult to understand the New Testament as a whole, and left the mind bewildered by its diversity."[2]

This wholesome recognition of an underlying unity has led to the production of many New Testament theologies organized along topical rather than along historical lines, which thus sometimes completely obscure the diversity and historical development of New Testament thought.[3] The inadequacy of the topical approach has been recently sensed by A. M. Hunter. When he wrote in 1944,[4] he recognized the "Dangers of Analysis" and saw the new approach altogether displacing the old analytical method. He expressed the hope that all future textbooks on New Testament theology would be written from this synthetic point of view. "Of the analytic textbooks with their series of 'separate compartment' chapters, each bearing its label—Synoptic, Pauline, Johannine, etc.—we have already more than enough."[5] In spite of this protest, when Hunter himself was asked to write a small introduction to New Testament theology, he resorted to the traditional structure to highlight the diversity of New Testament thought within its basic unity.[6]

We do not mean to accuse Prof. Hunter of inconsistency. On the contrary, we applaud his mature judgment of using a method which will bring out diversity without ignoring the integrating unity that Hunter finds in the "fact of Christ."[7]

The student of the New Testament must also be alert to the

---

[2] C. H. Dodd, *The Present Task in New Testament Studies* (1936), pp. 32ff.

[3] See the theologies by A. Richardson, F. V. Filson, and F. C. Grant. The same tendency is seen in Germany in the theology of E. Stauffer.

[4] *The Unity of the New Testament* (1944). Published in America under the title *The Message of the New Testament*.

[5] *Ibid.*, p. 121.

[6] A. M. Hunter, *Introducing New Testament Theology* (1957). The world of biblical studies is poorer because Hunter was not asked to write a major text rather than this brief handbook.

[7] *Ibid.*, pp. 9-10.

interaction between its thought development and its historical environment. Historically, the New Testament is the story of a movement from the Semitic to the Hellenistic world. The ministry of Jesus of Nazareth was carried out in Galilee and Judea among the Jews, and his language was that of first-century Judaism: Aramaic. His message was the proclamation of a thoroughly Jewish concern: the Kingdom of God. However, the entire New Testament is in Greek, and practically every book of the New Testament was addressed to or written for an audience in the Hellenistic world that was usually made up of people of Graeco-Roman culture. Furthermore, outside of the Synoptic Gospels, the Kingdom of God is distinctly a secondary concern.

The history of the gospel tradition is a history of the translation of a story from Aramaic into Greek, even though the earliest stages of this history are lost to us. Unavoidably, the Greek language determined to a substantial degree the formulation of the message. To what extent did Greek thought influence or modify the content? Does the variety in the New Testament writings reflect a progressive Hellenization of an original Jewish gospel? What do the Pauline justification by faith and the Johannine eternal life have in common with the Synoptic Kingdom of God?

The most extreme critics of the comparative religions school insist that such a historical development must be presupposed.[8] The historical Jesus is to be understood altogether in the context of first-century Judaism, as an apocalyptic prophet preaching the imminent end of the world. When the gospel moved out of its Jewish environment onto Greek soil, it began to be modified by Hellenistic influences, particularly that of Gnostic dualism. The Gnostic myth recounts the fate of the soul. It tells of its origin in the world of light, its tragic fall from the heavenly realm of light, its life as an alien on earth, its imprisonment in

[8] R. Bultmann, *Existence and Faith*, ed. Schubert Ogden (1960), pp. 52f.

11

the body, its deliverance and final ascent, and its return to the world of light. The soul—man's true, inner self—is a part, a splinter, a spark of a heavenly figure of light, the original man. This heavenly man comes to earth to deliver the imprisoned sparks of light and bring them back to their true heavenly home.[9]

Although Bultmann recognizes the contrast between this Gnostic view of man and the Christian message so far as it remained true to the tradition of the Old Testament and Judaism and the earliest church,[10] he believes that a syncretistic process began in which Gnostic thought influenced Christian thinking, particularly in such matters as eschatological dualism, the fall of creation, the heavenly redeemer figure, demonic world rulers, and emancipating knowledge.[11]

Coming from a scholar of such massive learning as Professor Bultmann, the argument for the syncretizing of the Christian gospel with Gnostic elements is impressive. However, a warning must be sounded. Our knowledge of the history of Gnosticism is still imprecise. A recent international congress of experts on Gnosticism even went so far as to appoint a study committee to solve the basic question of the definition of Gnosis and Gnosticism.[12] The theology of the fully developed Gnostic system of the second century A.D. is well known; but the history of the emergence of this dualistic system is obscure, particularly the extent to which one can speak of a pre-Christian Gnostic movement. Bultmann and the so-called comparative religions school (*religionsgeschichtliche Schule*) believe that Gnosticism was a pre-Christian syncretistic mythology that distinctly influenced the Christian faith in its formative stages. Others hold that while we may recognize pre-Christian gnosticizing tendencies, Gnosti-

---

[9] See R. Bultmann, *Primitive Christianity in Its Contemporary Setting* (1956), pp. 163f.

[10] *Theology of the New Testament* (1951), I, 168.

[11] *Ibid.* pp. 172ff.

[12] See the report by George MacRae, "Gnosis in Messina," *Catholic Biblical Quarterly*, XXVIII (1966), 322-333.

cism is a Christian heresy that emerged in the second century A.D.[13]

The Greek View

Until we can reconstruct with some confidence the emergence of Gnosticism, it is highly speculative to speak of the influence of Gnostic ideas on the emerging Christian faith. There is, however, a body of Greek literature that contains a view of man and the world very close to that of developed Gnosticism, namely, those Greek philosophical and religious writings that reflect the influence of Platonic dualism. These are writings that are well known and datable; and it is profitable to compare their view of man and the world with the biblical view in both the Old and New Testaments. Such a comparison leads to two conclusions: that the Greek view[14] of man and the world is different in kind from the biblical view; and that the unity and diversity of the several important strands of New Testament thought can be illustrated in terms of this contrast.

The basic problem is that of dualism. However, dualism means different things in the Greek view and in the biblical view.

The view found in Plato and in later thinkers, influenced by

[13] See R. McL. Wilson, *The Gnostic Problem* (1958), pp. 64ff.; G. Quispel, R. McL. Wilson, and H. Jonas, "Gnosticism and the New Testament," in *The Bible in Modern Scholarship,* ed. J. P. Hyatt (1965), pp. 252-293.

[14] We are deliberately using the expression, the "Greek view," in spite of Prof. Barr's protest against it (*Old and New in Interpretation* [1966], p. 39) because the Platonic dualism is roughly similar to Gnostic dualism, and the contemporary debate centers around the influence of this dualism on the New Testament. It is obvious, as Barr points out, that the Platonic view is not the only Greek view. Indeed, Guthrie says that Stoicism might be called the representative philosophy of the Hellenistic and Graeco-Roman ages (*A History of Greek Philosophy* [1962], I, 17). However, Stoic pantheistic materialism with its all-permeating divine fire is philosophically the opposite of dualism and plays no role in the current debate on syncretism. We shall show that the Platonic view was of wide currency in New Testament times; and in view of its later influence on Christian theology, we feel justified in calling it the Greek view.

him, is essentially the same cosmological dualism as is found in later Gnosticism. Like Gnosticism, Platonism is a dualism of two worlds, one the visible world and the other an invisible "spiritual" world. As in Gnosticism, man stands between these two worlds, related to both. Like Gnosticism, Platonism sees the origin of man's truest self (his soul) in the invisible world, whence his soul has fallen into the visible world of matter. Like Gnosticism, it sees the physical body as a hindrance, a burden, sometimes even as the tomb of the soul. Like Gnosticism, it conceives of salvation as the freeing of the soul from its entanglement in the physical world that it may wing its way back to the heavenly world. Two further elements found in Gnosticism do not appear in the Platonic philosophers: that matter is *ipso facto* the source of evil, and that redemption is accomplished by a heavenly redeemer who descends to earth to deliver the fallen souls and lead them back to heaven.

The biblical dualism is utterly different from this Greek view. It is religious and ethical, not cosmological. The world is God's world; man is God's creature, although rebellious, sinful and fallen. Salvation is achieved not by a flight from the world but by God's coming to man in his earthly, historical experience. Salvation never means flight from the world to God; it means, in effect, God's descent from heaven to bring man in historical experience into fellowship with himself. Therefore the consummation of salvation is eschatological. It does not mean the gathering of the souls of the righteous in heaven, but the gathering of a redeemed people on a redeemed earth in perfected fellowship with God. The theologies of the Synoptic Gospels, of John, and of Paul are to be understood in terms of this Hebrew dualism, and each of them stands in sharp contrast to the Greek dualism. The unifying element in New Testament theology is the fact of the divine visitation of men in the person and mission of Jesus Christ; diversity exists in the progressive unfolding of the meaning of this divine visitation and in the various ways the one revelatory, redeeming event is capable of being interpreted.

Since radical differences between Greek and Hebrew ways of thinking have recently been challenged,[15] we must now develop our thesis and document it in detail.

The foundations of the Greek view go back to the theology of the Orphic sect, which came to light in Greece in the sixth century B.C., and spread throughout the Greek world and into southern Italy, profoundly influencing Plato and later Greek thought. This theology is embodied in the ancient myth of Zagreus (Dionysus), begotten by Zeus of Demeter. Zagreus fell under the power of the Titans, wicked enemies of Zeus. In his effort to escape them, Zagreus changed himself into a bull; but the Titans captured him, tore him to pieces, and devoured him. However, Zeus blasted the Titans by a flash of lightning, and from their ashes arose the human race. Mankind thus possesses two elements: a divine element from Zagreus and a wicked element from the Titans. This mythology expresses the Orphic theology of the dualism of body and soul. Man must free himself from the Titanic elements and, purified, return to the gods, a fragment of whom is living in him. Expressed in other words, "man's duty is to free himself from the chains of the body in which the soul lies fast bound like the prisoner in his cell."[16] This freedom is not easily achieved. Usually the soul at death flutters free in the air, only to enter into a new body. It may pass through a series of deaths and reincarnations. Finally, by the sacred rites of the cult and by a life of ascetic purity, man may escape the wheel of birth and become divine.[17]

The main elements of this Orphic dualism appear in Plato's concept of man and the world. His cosmic dualism is paralleled by his anthropological dualism. The soul of man in his earthly existence is composite, consisting of the reasoning part or mind (*nous*), the spirited or courageous part (*thumos*), and the

[15] See James Barr, "Athens or Jerusalem?–The Question of Distinctiveness," in *Old and New in Interpretation* (1966), pp. 34-64.

[16] E. Rohde, *Psyche* (1925), p. 342.

[17] For Orphic doctrine, see Rohde, *op. cit.*, pp. 335-361; E. O. James in *Judaism and Christianity*, ed. W. O. E. Oesterley (1937), I, 43-46; W. K. C. Guthrie, *Orpheus and the Greek Religion* (1952).

appetitive part (*epithumia*). These three parts of the soul are located respectively in the head, the chest, and the midriff.[18] The highest part, mind, being divine and immortal, pre-existed before the creation of the body[19] and was made out of the same material as the soul of the universe by the Creator (Demiurge) himself.[20] The creation of the body and the two lower parts of the soul were entrusted to the young gods,[21] apparently to relieve the Demiurge of direct responsibility for evil. The lower parts of the soul, like the body, are mortal. Human experience is a struggle between the higher and lower parts of the soul. While Plato in this way locates moral evil in the soul, it is in that part of the soul that was created with the body and, like the body, is mortal. Most of the time, Plato speaks of the soul as simple in essence, and as the enemy of the body with its appetites and passions. "The soul is most like the divine and immortal and intellectual and indissoluble and unchanging, and the body, on the contrary, most like the human and mortal and multiform and unintellectual and dissoluble and ever-changing."[22] The soul partakes of the nature of the divine, which Plato understands to consist of such qualities as beauty, wisdom, and goodness,[23] which have objective existence in the realm of the invisible and incorporeal. The soul, then, belongs to the noumenal world and descends from this higher world into the phenomenal world of bodily existence whence it strives to regain its proper place in the higher world.

Plato likens this struggle to a charioteer driving two winged horses, one noble and the other ignoble. The noble horse wishes to mount up to the sky, to the realm of the divine eternal realities; it represents the divine immortal part of the soul whose

---

18 *Timaeus* 69D-70A; *Republic* 439-441.
19 See Plato's argument for pre-existence based on memory, *Phaedo* 72E.
20 For Plato's idea of God, see W. E. Greene, *Moira* (1948), pp. 286f., 291.
21 *Timaeus* 41C.
22 *Phaedo* 80B.
23 *Phaedrus* 246E.

16

proper realm is the region above the heaven of "the colourless, formless, and intangible truly existing essence [*ousia ontōs ousa*] with which all true knowledge is concerned."[24] The ignoble horse—the lower part of the soul—drags downward toward the earth, and, if it is not disciplined, corrupts the soul with impurities. "There the utmost toil and struggle await the soul."[25]

The body is thus the enemy of the soul, for it is a mass of evil,[26] and serves as a prison for the soul.[27] The body hinders the soul from the acquisition of knowledge.[28]

Plato stops short of thoroughgoing dualism of mind/matter,[29] in which matter is *ipso facto* evil as in later Gnosticism. "But Plato constantly . . . conjures up a sense of that inert, negative, imperfect kind of being which is opposed to mind or soul, to purpose or good, and which as such is a source of evil, or is indeed evil itself."[30] There is some kind of necessity (*anankē*) in matter which makes it intractable to goodness, reason, and mind.

In a real sense of the word, salvation for Plato is by knowledge. "Wherefore we should seek to escape hence [from this world] to that other world as speedily as we may; and the way of escape is by becoming like to God so far as we can; and the becoming like is becoming just and holy by taking thought" [*meta phroneseōs*].[31] Man's highest exercise is the cultivation of the mind and the control of the body; this is the object of the wise man, the philosopher. The mind can apprehend truth;

[24] *Phaedrus* 247C.
[25] *Ibid.* 247B.
[26] *Phaedo* 66B.
[27] *Ibid.* 82E; 62B; *Republic* 517B; *Cratylus* 400C. Plato considers the Pythagorean concept *sōma-sēma* (see also *Gorgias* 493A), and while he does not accept *sēma* (tomb) as an explanation for *sōma* (body), he does liken the body to a prison.
[28] *Phaedo* 66.
[29] In precision, we ought not speak of a "spiritual" world, for Plato does not use the word *pneuma* of the noumenal world; it is the world of forms or ideas that are beheld by the mind, the highest part of the soul.
[30] Greene, *Moira*, p. 302.
[31] *Theatetus* 176A (Greene's trans.); See *Moira*, p. 302.

but the bodily senses can hinder the soul from the acquisition of knowledge. Therefore the mind must have as little to do as possible with the body.[32] The philosopher despises all but the necessary bodily needs that he may devote himself to the soul.[33] The philosopher who succeeds in controlling the body and cultivating the mind will think thoughts that are immortal and divine. He lays hold on truth and partakes of immortality so far as that is possible. Those who attain this beatific[34] vision are loath to descend to human affairs, but their souls are ever hastening into the upper world in which they desire to dwell[35] because this escape from the earth is to become like God.[36] "When the soul inquires alone by itself, it departs into the realm of the pure, the everlasting, the immortal and the changeless, and being akin to these, it dwells always with them whenever it is by itself and is not hindered. . . . And this state of the soul is called wisdom."[37]

Upon death, the souls of such wise men and philosophers, having been purified from the body, depart to the realm of the noble, pure, invisible, and immortal, to the realm of the good and wise god, where in happiness and freedom from all human ills they will live in truth through all time with the gods.[38] The souls that were not purified but which loved the body with its appetites and were thus interpenetrated with the corporeal[39] must undergo a series of reincarnations, each suitable to the character of the individual's earthly existence.[40]

One further feature in Plato deserves attention because of its importance in Hellenistic philosophy. While reality is found only in the noumenal world and is apprehended by reason, by mind,

---

[32] *Phaedo* 65B.
[33] *Ibid.* 64D, 82C, 114E.
[34] *Timaeus* 90C.
[35] *Republic* 517D.
[36] *Theatetus* 176B.
[37] *Phaedo* 79D. See also *Phaedrus* 247.
[38] *Ibid.* 80D-81A.
[39] *Ibid.* 81B.
[40] *Phaedrus* 249. For further notes on the fate of impure souls, see Rohde, *Psyche*, pp. 481ff.

Plato can describe this experience of apprehending reality in mystical language. This is true of the experience of the soul in its pre-existent state, when it directly beholds the beauties of the world of reality.

> But at that former time they saw beauty shining in brightness, when with a blessed company—we following in the train of Zeus, and others in that of some other god—they saw the blessed sight and vision and were initiated into that which is rightly called the most blessed of mysteries, which we celebrated in a state of perfection, when we were without experience of the evils which awaited us in the time to come, being permitted as initiates to the sight of perfect and simple and calm and happy apparitions, which we saw in the pure light, being ourselves pure and not entombed in this which we carry about with us and call the body, in which we are imprisoned like an oyster in its shell.[41]

This noumenal world, from which the soul has descended into the realm of matter and of body, is a "region above the heaven" where

> the colourless, formless, and intangible truly existing essence with which all true knowledge is concerned, holds this region and is visible only to the mind, the pilot of the soul. Now the divine intelligence, since it is nurtured on mind and pure knowledge, and the intelligence of every soul which is capable of receiving that which befits it, rejoices in seeing reality for a space of time and by gazing upon truth is nourished and made happy until the revolution brings it again to the same place.[42]

Plato goes on to describe the philosopher who lives by reason—and so has mounted up to apprehend God—as one who has been "initiated into perfect mysteries," and who has become truly perfect in the sense of the mystery religions.[43]

[41] *Phaedrus* 250C.
[42] *Phaedrus* 248D.
[43] *Ibid.* 249C.

Are we to understand Plato as a mystic, as Kirk's treatment seems to suggest,[44] or did Plato use the language of contemporary religious experience to describe the critical faculty of reason? While such passages as those quoted are capable of the mystical interpretation, Plato's emphasis on mental discipline and the importance of education by which the young may be brought gradually to behold eternal and absolute truths and values suggests that he is using popular religious terminology to describe the faculty of reason.[45] The mystical element emerges clearly in neo-Platonism; whether or not it is important in Plutarch and Philo is another question.

Aristotle has a different view of the soul than Plato, which we need only note in passing because the Platonic view exercised far wider influence in the New Testament world than did the Aristotelian. Aristotle did not accept Plato's concept of the noumenal world of ideas, and along with it, he rejected the conception of the pre-existence of the soul. The *psyche* has no existence apart from the body, for the two form an indivisible unity. Therefore there is neither pre-existence nor immortality of the individual soul. Aristotle does accept the Platonic idea of a division in the soul. Mind, the rational part of the soul, is immortal and eternal, and comes to man from outside and returns at death.[46] However, this mind is not personal and individual, and there is no personal immortality in Aristotle.[47]

The influence and prevalence of the Platonic dualism may be realized by the fact that it is found in widely different quarters in New Testament times. We refer here only to two: the Greek Plutarch and the Jew Philo.

Plutarch provides us with a vivid picture of the state of Greek religion in educated circles in the late first century. He was thoroughly nurtured in Greek thought, culture, and religion, and

[44] K. E. Kirk, *The Vision of God* (1932), pp. 23ff. Kirk does not discuss the nature of Plato's "vision of God."

[45] See F. Copleston, *A History of Philosophy* (1962), I, 1, 186f., 225ff.

[46] *De anima* I, 430a.10ff., 736b.27, 408b.12-30.

[47] See E. D. Burton, *Spirit, Soul and Flesh* (1918), pp. 41-48.

his chief aim was to harmonize traditional Greek religion with Greek philosophy, represented primarily by Plato,[48] and to avoid the twin evils of atheism and superstition. We cannot give here a comprehensive treatment of Plutarch's thought,[49] but we shall only illustrate by his work the persistence of Platonic dualism in the Hellenistic world. The heart of Plutarch's philosophical thought is the same cosmological and anthropological dualism found in Plato, tied together with Hellenistic cosmology.

In his dialogue *The Face of the Moon* we find an eschatological myth about human destiny.[50] Man consists of body and soul, but the soul is itself complex, consisting of soul and mind.[51] Only mind is immortal, although the soul survives the death of the body. After this death, man's mind-soul must spend time in a sort of Hades, which occupies the space between the earth and the moon. Here man must die a second death, when the soul is gently and slowly purged so that man is finally reduced to his one immortal part—mind alone. This purifying process consists in purging away the pollutions that were contracted from the body. This process of purification is neither uniform nor uniformly successful. Some souls succeed in purging away all of the evil influences of the body, that is, in making the irrational element in the soul completely subordinate to reason. Other souls are so laden with evils from bodily existence that the purification is incomplete and they fall back again to earth to be reborn in different bodies. Those who achieve purification and gain a firm foothold on the moon are converted into daemons

[48] M. Nilsson, *Geschichte der griechischen Religion* (1961), II, 402f.
[49] There is a serious lack of up-to-date works on Plutarch in English. See John Oakesmith, *The Religion of Plutarch* (1902); T. R. Glover, *The Conflict of Religions in the Roman Empire* (1909), pp. 75-112.
[50] *Face of the Moon*, 940F-945D. All references to Plutarch are to the fifteen volumes of the Loeb edition, which is very serviceable because of the continuous numbering employed throughout the volumes.
[51] Elsewhere Plutarch reflects Plato's idea of the pre-existence of the soul and an epistemology of knowledge of life in this former existence. See *Consolation to his Wife*, 611E. "Its most generous fault [viz. of old age] is to render the soul stale in its memories of the other world and make it cling tenaciously to this one."

21

—a race of disembodied souls who serve as intermediaries between God and men.[52]

Here we have the same elements we have found in Plato's dualism: two worlds, the phenomenal or material, and the conceptual;[53] a complex soul with the mind as its highest and most divine faculty;[54] the body as a source of evil and pollution to the mind;[55] this world as an alien place from which the soul must escape to find its true destiny;[56] salvation consisting of purification from the pollution incurred in bodily life and the freeing of the mind from bodily and worldly evil.[57] The disembodied souls that have become daemons are not yet perfected; they can fall back and be reborn on earth. Final destiny is to be released from the cycle of birth[58] and to attain a permanent place in the heavenly realm.

Plutarch no more regards matter as evil *ipso facto* than did

[52] This same mythology is found with more elaborate detail in *Divine Vengeance* 560F-567E, and *The Sign of Socrates* 590A-594A.

[53] *Isis and Osiris* 373F. Osiris lives "far removed from the earth, uncontaminated and unpolluted and pure from all matter that is subject to destruction and death." While the souls of men are "compassed about by bodies and emotions," they can have only a dim vision of the heavenly world. "But when these souls are set free and migrate into the realm of the invisible and the unseen, the dispassionate and the pure, then this god becomes their leader."

[54] See *Isis and Osiris* 353A; 371A. Intelligence is the eye of the soul. *Divine Vengeance* 563E.

[55] *E at Delphi* 432A.

[56] In *Consolation to His Wife* 611E, Plutarch says that the soul is imperishable. It is like a captive bird that can become so tamed by this life and bodily existence that upon escaping the body at death, it alights again and re-enters the body, and does not leave off or cease from becoming entangled in the passions and fortunes of this world through repeated births. In *Divine Vengeance* 590, the soul is released from the body and finds great relief in being set free from the confines of bodily existence.

[57] *Obsolescence of Oracles* 415B-C; *E at Delphi* 432C. Disembodied souls that succeed in rising above the bodily passions rise to heaven, "shaking off a sort of dimness and darkness as one might shake off mud" (*Divine Vengeance* 591F).

[58] *Divine Vengeance* 590C.

Plato.[59] The material world is, nevertheless, the sphere of evil and is evil in its functioning.[60] The evil nature of the world is further reflected in his idea of God and God's relationship to the world. God is described in philosophical language[61] and also in terms of mind and reason.[62] He cannot come into direct contact with the evil world or be the author of anything evil.[63] At the same time, Plutarch's God is described in eclectic terms; he is the supreme being who is worshipped everywhere by different peoples under different names.[64]

Plutarch fills the void between God and the world by two ranks of intermediaries: the traditional Greek gods[65] and the order of disembodied souls that have succeeded in achieving purification from the pollution of bodily earthly existence: the daemons.[66] These daemons are, obviously, very different from

[59] The evil element is "formlessness and disarrangement" (*Obsolescence of Oracles* 428F); evil is "innate, in large amount, in the body and elsewhere in the soul of the universe" (*Isis and Osiris* 371A). Elsewhere, the material world is not evil but "orphaned, incomplete, and good for nothing, unless there be an animating soul to make use of it" (*E at Delphi* 390E). Plutarch does attribute to Plato the view that matter is evil (*Obsolescence of Oracles* 414F).

[60] "Nature must have in herself the source and origin of evil, just as she contains the source and origin of good" (*Isis and Osiris* 369D).

[61] "What, then, really is Being? It is that which is eternal, without beginning and without end, to which no length of time brings change" (*E at Delphi* 392E-393C). God is free from emotion and activity (*Obsolescence of Oracles* 420E).

[62] "God gives to men . . . of sense and intelligence [*nous kai phronēsis*] . . . only a share, inasmuch as these are his especial possessions and his sphere of activity. For the Deity is blessed . . . through knowledge and intelligence" (*Isis and Osiris* 351D).

[63] *Isis and Osiris* 369B.

[64] *Isis and Osiris* 377F-378A.

[65] Plutarch regards the Stoic denial of the existence of these gods to be atheism; and one of his main objectives is to preserve traditional belief in these gods.

[66] *Isis and Osiris* 360Eff. Daemons are souls of men which do not yet possess the divine [*to theion*] unmixed and uncontaminated, but also have a portion of the nature of the soul and the perceptive faculties of the body. Not only can men become daemons; daemons can also become gods (*Obsolescence of Oracles* 415B), and daemons can fall back into human existence again.

the demons of the Semitic world and should not be confused with them. The former are the disembodied souls of men in the process of redemption from the material world; the latter are evil superhuman spirits that belong to an invisible world and are hostile to both God and men. The biblical God can and does act directly and immediately in nature and in history, although he may sometimes employ angels as his emissaries. Plutarch's God cannot be brought directly into men's emotions and activities nor dragged down to human needs. It is the daemons, not God, who are present at the mysteries and sacred rites.[67] God uses the daemons both to communicate his will to men and to receive communications from men.[68]

On one occasion, Plutarch solves the problem of evil with a different kind of dualism. God cannot be the author of evil, yet evil exists in the material world. Plutarch appeals to the Zoroastrian idea of two ultimate principles or two gods—one good, the other evil,[69] and he mistakenly attributes to Plato the idea of an evil world-soul.[70] Plutarch concludes that if there are two ultimate opposing principles, they are not of equal strength but the predominance rests with the better.[71]

Salvation for Plutarch means the mastery of the bodily appetites and passions by the rule of reason or mind, which will lead to a blessed immortality in the afterlife. This is accomplished by purification, by participation in the religious rites of traditional Greek religion,[72] but it can also be described as salvation by knowledge.[73]

---

[67] *Obsolescence of Oracles* 416F-417A.

[68] *E at Delphi* 416F; *Isis and Osiris* 361C.

[69] *Isis and Osiris* 370A-C.

[70] *Ibid.* 370F. See his appeal to two ultimate first principles in *Obsolescence of Oracles* 428F-429B.

[71] *Isis and Osiris* 371A.

[72] *Isis and Osiris* 351C.

[73] "Nothing . . . is more divine than reasoning [*logos*], and especially reasoning about the gods; and nothing has a greater influence toward happiness" (*Isis and Osiris* 378C). To rule pleasure by reason is the mark of the wise man; the life of physical pleasures is dissolute and bestial (*Education of Children* 8). Wisdom is the knowledge of the

We may appreciate the extent to which Platonic dualistic thinking influenced the Hellenistic world by tracing its basic structure in the Jew Philo of Alexandria. Philo provides us with an excellent illustration of syncretism. His purpose was to commend his Jewish faith to the contemporary world of Greek thought, and this he does by his famed allegorical method of interpreting the Old Testament. He remained a thoroughgoing Jew in that he believed the Old Testament to be the Word of God, in which God had revealed himself; and he remained a steadfast adherent of the Mosaic law. But Philo's allegorical method made it possible for him to find thoroughly Greek ideas in the Jewish Scriptures. As Armstrong put it, in his interpretation of Genesis, he treats the creation account more like a Platonic myth than as a record of events that really happened.[74]

In this way it comes about that in his cosmology and anthropology Philo is a Greek rather than a Jew. To illustrate: the meaning of the statement that a man leaves his father and mother and cleaves to his wife so that the two become one (Gen. 2:24) is not the intimate relationship between a man and a woman. Rather, it refers to the mind that has been perverted from its true occupation of contemplating the world of invisible realities to become enslaved by the sense perceptions of the body. One of Philo's main concerns is to find this Platonic dualism of mind and body in the law of Moses by the use of allegory.

The voluminous writings of Philo are lacking in logical structure, and his ideas must be documented at length from the great

---

gods; the soul by her innate power can grasp the good. Such is the nature of virtue, truth, and beauty as well as of geometry and astronomy (*Love of Wealth* 528A; *The Myth of Timarchus*). In the *Divine Vengeance* 591D-F, Plutarch discusses the "salvation" of the soul in terms of the rule of mind over the passions of the body. "The effort to arrive at the truth, and especially the truth about the gods, is a longing for the divine" (*Isis and Osiris* 351E).

[74] A. H. Armstrong, *An Introduction to Ancient Philosophy* (1949), p. 160.

variety of his works. For our purpose, we shall summarize the elements of Philo's view of the world and the soul by a single quotation compiled from his work *On the Giants,* and enlarge upon it by additional citations.

It is Moses' custom to give the name of angels to those whom other philosophers call demons, souls that is which fly and hover in the air. Now some of the souls have descended into bodies, but others have never deigned to be brought into union with any parts of the earth. They are consecrated and devoted to the service of the Father and Creator whose wont it is to employ them as ministers and helpers, to have charge and care of mortal man. But the others descending into the body as though into a stream have sometimes been caught in the swirl of its rushing torrent and swallowed up thereby, at other times have been able to stem the current, have risen to the surface and then soared upwards back to the place from whence they came. These last, then, are the souls of those who have given themselves to genuine philosophy, who from first to last study to die to the life of the body, that a higher existence immortal and incorporeal in the presence of Him who is Himself immortal and uncreate, may be their portion. But the souls which have sunk beneath the stream, are the souls of the others who have held no account of wisdom. They have abandoned themselves to the unstable things of chance, none of which has aught to do with our noblest part, the soul or mind, but all are related to that dead thing which was our birth-fellow, the body, or to objects more lifeless still, glory, wealth, and offices and honours, and all other illusions which like images or pictures are created through the deceit of false opinion by those who have never gazed upon true beauty (12-15). . . . The chief cause of ignorance is the flesh, and the tie which binds us so closely to the flesh (29). . . . Nothing thwarts its growth so much as our fleshly nature (30). . . . For souls that are free from flesh and body spend their days in the theatre of the universe and with a joy that none can hinder see and hear things divine, which they have desired with love insatiable. But those which bear the burden of the flesh, oppressed by the grievous load, cannot look up to the heavens as they revolve, but with necks bowed downwards are constrained to stand rooted to the ground like four-footed beasts (31).

Here are most of the salient elements of Philo's dualism. By virtue of the fact that man consists of two parts—soul and body—he belongs to two worlds: heaven and earth. Thus man exists in the borderland between the mortal and the immortal, being mortal in respect to his visible part, the body, and immortal in respect to the invisible part, the mind.[75] Souls are pre-existent, belonging to the world of angels. Angels are disembodied souls inhabiting the air. They never descend into bodies, and they serve God as intermediaries toward men. Human beings are souls that have descended from heaven and entered into bodies of flesh. Elsewhere Philo says that at the creation of the body, there is created also a lower, irrational part of the soul, which, like the body, is mortal. The substance of the lower or irrational part of the soul, which man shares with the irrational animals, is blood; the substance of the higher part of the soul is the divine spirit that God breathed into man at his creation.[76] Thus man finds himself in conflict between the higher and lower parts of his being—between the soul-mind and the body, or between the rational soul that is mind and the irrational part of the soul. There are two kinds of men: those who live by reason—the divine inbreathing, and those who live by blood and the pleasure of the flesh.[77]

Philo often speaks of the body as the enemy of the soul. While he does not recognize matter *ipso facto* as evil,[78] the body

---

[75] *Op. mundi.* 135.
[76] *Quis rer. div. heres* 55-56; *Spec. Leg.* IV, 122-3.
[77] *Quis rer. div. heres* 57.
[78] "It almost seems that Philo regards matter as evil." R. McL. Wilson, *The Gnostic Problem* (1958), p. 45.

27

is a foul prison-house of the soul,[79] like a sackcloth robe,[80] a tomb (*sēma*),[81] a grave (*trumbos*).[82]

Some souls "sink beneath the stream" of bodily materiality, so that the vision of the heavenly is lost. But those who pursue wisdom and philosophy, namely, God, those who discipline the body and cultivate the mind, "soar upwards" to behold the wonders of the heavenly realm. Philo describes this experience of "salvation" in the language of the Greek mysteries as though it involved ecstatic vision.

> For when the mind soars aloft and is being initiated in the mysteries of the Lord, it judges the body to be wicked and hostile. . . . The philosopher, being enamored of the noble thing that lives in himself, cares for the soul, and pays no regard to that which is really a corpse, the body, concerned only that the best part of him, his soul, may not be hurt by an evil thing, a very corpse, tied to it. . . . When, then, O soul, wilt thou in fullest measure realize thyself to be a corpse-bearer? Will it not be when thou art perfected and accounted worthy of prizes and crowns? For then shalt thou be no lover of the body, but a lover of God. . . . For when the mind has carried off the rewards of victory, it condemns the corpse-body to death.[83]

Since the highest or rational part of the soul is the mind, in a real sense of the word salvation is by knowledge—knowledge of the heavenly world and God and a correct understanding of the nature of this world.

> For it will befit those who have entered into comradeship with knowledge to desire to see the Existent if they may, but, if they cannot, to see at any rate his image, the most

---

[79] *De Migr. Abr.* 8
[80] *Quis rer. div. heres* 54
[81] *L.A.* I, 108; *Spec. Leg.* IV, 188.
[82] *Quod Deus sit Imm.* 148.
[83] *L.A.* III, 71-74.

holy word [*logos*], and after the word its most perfect work of all that our senses know, even the world. For by philosophy nothing else has ever been meant, than the earnest desire to see these things exactly as they are.[84]

For there are two things of which we consist, soul and body. The body, then, has been formed out of earth, but the soul is of the upper air, a particle detached from the deity [*apospasma theion*]. . . . The soul being a portion of an ethereal nature has . . . ethereal and divine food; for it is fed by knowledge [*epistemē*] in its various forms and not by meat and drink, of which the body stands in need.[85]

This direct apprehension of reality by the mind is closely analogous to Plato's theory of knowledge, with one important difference: Knowledge for Plato is either dialectic reasoning or recollection of what the soul has known in its pre-existent state. For this pre-existent knowledge or dialectic reasoning, Philo substitutes prophecy, revelation in the law of Moses.[86] The tension between the Jew and the Greek in Philo is seen in the fact that he sometimes speaks of the immediate vision of God by the soul.[87] But when he speaks more reflectively about the meaning of the vision of God, the Greek takes over, and he cannot speak of a direct vision of God himself but only of the existence of God. "It is impossible that the God who is should be perceived at all by created beings. . . . For it is quite enough for a man's reasoning faculty to advance so far as to learn that the Cause of the universe is and subsists [*esti kai huparchei*]." The powers of God at work in the world "make evident not his essence [*ousia*] but his subsistence [*huparxis*] from the things which he accomplishes."[88]

[84] *Conf. Ling.* 97.
[85] *L.A.* III, 161.
[86] See H. A. Wolfson, *op. cit.*, I, 8ff., 85ff.
[87] Those who pursue the contemplative life, the "sight of the soul," alone are able to gain knowledge of truth and falsehood. They "desire the vision of the Existent and soar above the sin of our senses" (*De Vita Cont.* 11).
[88] *De Post. Caini* 168-9. See also *Mut. Nom.* 9-10.

We cannot here discuss the interesting question of whether Philo was primarily a mystic or a philosopher. Are we to interpret his language about vision and ecstasy and corybantic frenzy literally and understand Philo to be the proponent of a Jewish mystery religion,[89] or are we to interpret such language somewhat figuratively and understand Philo to be more a philosopher than a mystic?[90] We feel that Philo is somewhat better understood as a philosopher than a mystic; but as we have pointed out, knowledge for him is not so much dialectical reasoning as it is human response to the divine revelation given in the law of Moses.

In any case, this knowledge of the world and of God, the ability to see things as they really are, leads to the salvation of the soul after death, which means the flight of the soul from this world to return to its true home in heaven. God's promise to Jacob to bring him back to the land he was leaving in Genesis 28:15

> hints at the doctrine of the immortality of the soul: for, as was said a little before, it forsook its heavenly abode and came into the body as into a foreign land. But the Father who gave it birth says that he will not permanently disregard it in its imprisonment, but will take pity on it and loose it from its chains, and escort it in freedom and safety to its mother-city.[91]

The rational part of the soul, which was pre-existent, is incorruptible and immortal,[92] and at death "removes its habitation

---

[89] See W. Bousset, *Die Religion des Judentums im späthellenistischen Zeitalter* (1906), pp. 438-455; E. R. Goodenough, *An Introduction to Philo Judaeus* (1962); *By Light, Light. The Mystic Gospel of Hellenistic Judaism* (1935); H. R. Willoughby, *Pagan Regeneration* (1929), pp. 225-262.

[90] H. A. Wolfson, *Philo, Foundation of Religious Philosophy in Judaism, Christianity, and Islam* (1948), 2 vols.

[91] *De Som.* I. 181.

[92] *Athanatos, Immut.* 10, 46; *aphthartos, Prob.* 7, 46; *Congr.* 97; *Spec.* I, 81.

from the mortal body and returns as if to the mother-city, from which it originally moved its habitation to this place."[93] This native home of the soul to which it returns after death is the heavens, where it rejoins the angels, who are pure souls who have never entered into bodies.[94] There is no trace of the idea of the resurrection of the body in Philo. The destiny of men is not a redeemed society living on a transformed earth; it is the flight of the soul from earth to heaven. In this basic thinking about man and his destiny, Philo is quite Greek and Platonic.

The Old Testament View

The Old Testament view of God, man, and the world is very different from Greek dualism. Fundamental to Hebrew thought is the belief that God is the creator, that the world is God's creation and is therefore in itself good. The Greek idea that the material world is the sphere of evil and a burden or a hindrance to the soul is alien to the Old Testament. When God created the world, he saw that it was good (Gen. 1:31). The world was created for God's glory (Ps. 19:1); the ultimate goal and destiny of creation is to glorify and praise its creator (Ps. 98:7-9). The Hebrews had no concept of nature; to them the world was the scene of God's constant activity. Thunder was the voice of God (Ps. 29:3, 5); pestilence is the heavy hand of the Lord (I Sam. 5:6); human life is the breath of God inbreathed in man's face (Gen. 2:7; Ps. 104:29).

To be sure, the world is not all it ought to be. Something has gone wrong. But the evil is not found in materiality, but in human sin. In creation, God displayed his goodness by making man the chief of all his creatures and by subjecting the created world to man's care (Gen. 1:28), entrusting to him dominion over all other creatures. When man in proud self-assertion refused to accept the role of creaturehood, when he succumbed to the temptation to "be like God" (Gen. 3:5) and fell into

[93] *Quaes. in Gen.* III, 11.
[94] H. A. Wolfson, *op. cit.*, I, 359-404.

31

sin, God placed the curse of death upon man and the burden of decay and evil upon the entire world, so that man might be continually reminded of the fundamental fact that sin disrupts the enjoyment of God's gifts, even in the physical realm. Life and happiness are God's gifts; pain, toil and death are the toll of sin.

The Old Testament never views the earth as an alien place nor as an indifferent theater on which man lives out his temporal life while seeking a heavenly destiny. Man and the world together belong to the order of creation; and in a real sense of the word, the world participates in man's fate. The world is affected by man's sin. Although the world was designed to reflect the divine glory and still does so, it is a tainted glory because of sin. This intimate relationship is sometimes expressed poetically. Because of human wickedness, "the land mourns, and all who dwell in it languish, and also the beasts of the field and the birds of the air and even the fish of the sea are taken away" (Hos. 4:3).

Behind this concept of man and the world is the theology that both man and the world are God's creation, and that man's true life consists in complete obedience to and dependence upon God. This can be illustrated by the Old Testament concept of life. There is no antithesis between physical and spiritual life, between the outer and the inner dimensions in man, between the lower and higher realms. Life is viewed in its wholeness as the full enjoyment of all of God's gifts. Some Christian theologies would consider this crassly materialistic; but a profound theology underlies it. Life, which can be enjoyed only from the perspective of obedience to God and love for him (Deut. 30:6), means physical prosperity, productivity (Deut. 30:9), a long life (Ps. 34:12; 91:16), bodily health and well-being (Prov. 4:22; 9:23; 22:4), physical security (Deut. 8:1); in brief, the enjoyment of all of God's gifts (Ps. 103:1-5). However, the enjoyment of these good things by themselves cannot be called life, for life means the enjoyment of God's gifts *in fellowship with God*. It is God alone who is the source of all good things, including life itself (Ps. 36:9). Those who forsake the Lord will be put to shame, for they have abandoned the fountain of life (Jer. 17:13). While health and bodily well-being are included in life, man does not live by bread alone; and the enjoyment of God's gifts apart from obedience to the word of God is not life (Deut. 8:3). Life, therefore, can be simply defined as the enjoyment of God's gifts *in fellowship with the God who gives them.* God alone has the way of life; it is only in his presence that there is fullness of joy and everlasting pleasures (Ps. 16:11).

Behind this understanding of life is a profound theology. Man shares with nature the fact of creaturehood. But man stands apart from all other creatures in that he was created in the image of God. For this reason, he enjoys a relationship to God different from that of all other creatures. However, this does not mean that men will ever transcend creaturehood. Indeed, the very root of sin is unwillingness to acknowledge the reality and implications of creaturehood. The fact that man is a physical creature in the world is neither the cause nor the measure of his sinfulness and thus a state from which he must be delivered. Sin does not result from the body's burdening down the soul or clouding the mind; it results from rebellion of the will, the self. The acceptance of man's creaturehood, the confession of complete and utter dependence upon the Creator God, is essential to man's true existence. Man truly knows himself, recognizes his true self, only when he realizes that he is God's creature. Then he accepts the humble role of one whose very life is contingent upon God's faithfulness and whose chief joy is to serve and worship his Creator. The root of sin is found not in succumbing to the physical side of his being, but in the intent to lift himself out of his creaturehood, to exalt himself above God, to refuse to give God the worship, praise, and obedience that are his due.

For this perspective salvation does not mean deliverance from creaturehood, for it is an essential and permanent element of man's essential being. For this reason the Old Testament never

33

pictures ultimate redemption as a flight from the world or escape from earthly, bodily existence. Salvation does not consist of freeing the soul from its engagement in the material world. On the contrary, ultimate redemption will involve the redemption of the whole man and of the world to which man belongs. This is the theology behind the doctrine of bodily resurrection, which only begins to emerge in the Old Testament[95] but which is clearly developed in Judaism and the New Testament.

The same basic theology is seen everywhere in the prophets in their hope of the redemption of the world. While the prophets in only a few places speak of resurrection (e.g., Isa. 25:8; Ezek. 37; Dan. 12:2), they constantly look forward to the consummation of God's redemptive purpose on a transformed earth. The nature of this transformation is diversely described. Sometimes the new world is depicted simply in terms of material abundance. The land will become so fruitful that there will be no lapse between the seasons. The grape harvest will be so prolific that the hills will be inundated in rivers of wine. War and devastation will be replaced by peace and security (Amos 9:13-15). On other occasions the transformation will be more radical. Isaiah describes it as new heavens and a new earth (65:17; 66:22), where premature death will be banished, peace and security enjoyed, and the curse of violence lifted from nature. "The wolf and the lamb shall feed together, the lion shall eat straw like an ox. They shall not hurt or destroy in all my holy mountain, says the Lord" (Isa. 65:25).[96]

The world is to be redeemed from its bondage to evil not by any process of gradual evolution nor through any powers resident in the world, but by a mighty act of God—a divine visitation. Some scholars have held that two different kinds of eschatology are to be found in Judaism: an authentic prophetic Hebrew hope that looks for an earthly kingdom arising out of history, and a dualistic hope that resulted from despair of his-

---

[95] See R. Martin-Achard, *From Death to Life* (1960), pp. 206ff.

[96] For a detailed discussion of the problems involved in this hope, see the present author's *Jesus and the Kingdom* (1964), chap. II.

tory as the scene of God's Kingdom and in its place looked for a transcendental order to be inaugurated by an irruption into history of the heavenly order. We believe this critical theory to be unsupported by our sources, and we have argued at length that the prophetic hope never looks for the establishment of God's Kingdom to result from forces imminent within history but only by a divine visitation—an irruption from outside into history.[97] Even in the oldest conceptions, God's kingship could be absolutely established only at the cost of a great change that would make an end of the present state of things and witness the establishment of something new. "There is no eschatology without rupture."[98] In the careful words of H. H. Rowley, the Day of the Lord was conceived "as the time of the divine in-breaking into history in spectacular fashion. While God was believed to be always active of the plane of history, using nature and men to fulfill his ends, the Day of the Lord was thought of as a day of more direct and clearly manifest action."[99]

While the prophets looked forward to a final visitation of God to redeem both God's people and the physical world, they were not pessimistic about the nature of historical existence before the coming of the Day of the Lord. One of the wholesome emphases of modern biblical theology is the acting of God in history. G. Ernest Wright has promoted the view that biblical theology is the recital of the redeeming and judicial acts of God in history;[100] and perhaps the greatest contemporary work on Old Testament theology—that of Gerhard von Rad—is a theology of the *kerygma*: the proclamation of the mighty deeds of God in history. James Barr has provided a healthy emendation of the view by insisting that in the thought of the Old Testament revelation does not occur in events alone but also in words.[101]

[97] *Ibid.*
[98] E. Jacob, *Theology of the Old Testament* (1958), p. 318.
[99] H. H. Rowley, *The Growth of the Old Testament* (1950), p. 139.
[100] Wright, *God Who Acts* (1952).
[101] James Barr, "Revelation through History in the Old Testament," *Interpretation*, XVII (1963), 193-205; "Concepts of History and Revelation," in *Old and New in Interpretation* (1966), pp. 65-102.

Von Rad recognizes that the acts and the words belong together. "History becomes word, and word becomes history."[102] Several years ago, the present author expounded a similar view. God does reveal himself in events; but the events do not speak for themselves. Their inner meaning must be set forth in words. Thus revelation occurs in an event-word complex, the prophetic interpreting word being an integral part of the event.[103]

Back of this concept of revelation is a profound theology of God: a living, personal God who is known to man because he chooses to reveal himself by visiting man in history. The God of the Old Testament is always "the God who comes."[104] "Let the floods clap their hands; let the hills sing for joy together—before the Lord, for he comes to rule the earth" (Ps. 98:8). "The Lord came from Sinai, and dawned from Seir upon us; he shone forth from Mount Paran, he came from the ten thousands of holy ones, with flaming fire at his right hand" (Deut. 33:2). "For behold, the Lord is coming forth out of his place, and will come down and tread upon the high places of the earth. And the mountains will melt under him and the valleys will be cleft like wax before the fire, like waters poured down a steep place" (Mic. 1:3-4). He came to Israel in Egypt to make them his people; he came to them again and again in their history; he will come again in a final eschatological visitation in the future to judge wickedness and to establish his Kingdom.[105]

For our present purpose, the important thing to note is the difference between the Hebrew and the Greek views of reality. For the Greek, the world, nature, human history—in sum, the sphere of the visible—formed the realm of flux and change, of becoming, of the transient. Reality belonged to the realm of the

---

[102] G. von Rad, *Old Testament Theology* (1965), II, p. 358.

[103] See G. E. Ladd, "The Saving Acts of God," *Basic Christian Doctrines*, ed. C. F. H. Henry (1962), pp. 7-13. See also "How is the Bible the Word of God?" in *The New Testament and Criticism* (1967), pp. 19-33.

[104] Cf. Georges Pidoux, *Le Dieu qui vient* (1947).

[105] For a development of this theme, see *Jesus and the Kingdom*, pp. 42-48.

invisible, the good, the unchanging, which could be apprehended only by the mind of the soul transcending the visible. Thus salvation was found in the flight of the soul from the world to the invisible world of God.

For the Hebrew, reality was found in God who makes himself known in the ebb and flow of both nature and historical events by his acts and by his words. God comes to men in their earthly experience. Thus the final redemption is not flight from this world to another world; it may be described as the descent of the other world—God's world—resulting in a transformation of this world.

The contrast between the Greek and Hebrew views of God and the world is reinforced further by the Old Testament anthropology. Hebrew man is not like the Greek man—a union of soul and body and thus related to two worlds. He is flesh animated by God's breath (*ruach*), who is thus constituted a living soul (*nephesh*) (Gen. 2:7; 7:22). *Nephesh* (soul) is not a part of man; it is man himself viewed as a living creature. *Nephesh* is life, both of men (Ex. 21:23; Ps. 33:19) and of animals (Prov. 12:10). If *nephesh* is man as a living creature, it can be used for man himself and indicate man as a person,[106] and also become a synonym for "I," "myself."[107] By an easy extension, *nephesh* is man seen in terms of his appetites and desires (Eccl. 6:2, 7) or in terms of his emotions or thoughts (Hos. 4:8; Ps. 35:25; Gen. 34:8; Ps. 139:14; Prov. 19:2).

If *nephesh* is man's life, it can be said to depart at death (Gen. 35:18; I Kings 17:21) or return if a person revives (I Kings 17:22). If the *nephesh* stands for man himself, it can be said that his *nephesh* departs to the underworld or *sheol* at death (Pss. 16:10; 30:3; 94:7). However, the Old Testament does not conceive of disembodied souls existing in the under-

---

[106] See Gen. 14:21; Ex. 16:16; Num. 5:6; Ezek. 33:6 (RSV, "any one"); Deut. 24:7 (RSV, "one"); Gen. 46:18 (sixteen "persons"). See Rev. 18:13 for this use.

[107] Ps. 34:2; Gen. 27:35, lit., "that my soul may bless you"; Jer. 3:11, "herself" equals "her soul."

world after departing from the body, as do Homer and other early Greek writers.[108] The Old Testament does not see *souls* in sheol, but shades (*rephaim*), which are a sort of pale replica of man as a living creature.[109] These shades are not altogether different from Homer's souls in Hades, and both represent a common conviction of natural theology, namely, that death is not the end of human existence, but that life in its fullness must be bodily life.

However, in following the course of their development, the Greek and the Hebrew thought sharply diverge. The Greeks, as we have seen, came to believe that there was something divine about the soul and that it must find release from bodily existence to take its flight to the stars. Hebrew thought developed very differently. There began to emerge, even in the Old Testament, the conviction that if men enjoy fellowship with God in life, this fellowship could not be broken by death. "For thou dost not give me [lit., my soul] up to sheol, or let thy godly one see the pit. Thou dost show me the path of life; in thy presence there is fullness of joy, in thy right hand are pleasures forevermore" (Ps. 16:10-11). "But God will ransom my soul from the power of sheol, for he will receive me" (Ps. 49:15). "Thou dost guide me with thy counsel, and afterward thou wilt receive me to glory" (Ps. 73:24). While such sayings hardly provide us with material for a doctrine of the intermediate state, they do express the undying conviction of the "imperishable blessedness of the man who lives in God."[110] They cannot conceive of this fellowship being broken, even by death. As Martin-Achard says, "Without actually being aware of it, the *Hasidim* are battering the gates of the kingdom of the dead; without reaching the positive assertion of the immortality or resurrection of the believer . . . they are preparing the way for future generations to proclaim that death is impotent against those who are living in

---

108 *Iliad* I. 3; *Odyssey* XI. 205. See E. D. Burton, *Spirit, Soul and Flesh* (1918), pp. 26ff.

109 See Job 26:5; Ps. 88:10; Prov. 9:18; Isa. 14:9; 26:19.

110 R. Martin-Achard, *From Death to Life* (1960), p. 165.

communion with the living God."[111] Later Judaism developed the idea of an intermediate state and sometimes identified the dead as souls, or conceived of the soul as existing after death.[112] However, unless there is Greek influence, as in the Wisdom of Solomon (8:19), the continuing existence of the soul in sheol is not due to some intrinsic quality of immortality which it shares with God but to the conviction that since God is the living God and master of both life and death, there must be a blessed destiny for individuals as well as for the nation. Almost always in Judaism, the individual hope finds its realization in bodily resurrection. In only a few places do we find the idea of a blessed immortality of the soul in heaven.[113]

We may now summarize our findings as to the difference between the basic Greek and Hebrew dualism. Greek dualism is that of two worlds, the visible and the invisible, the phenomenal and the noumenal, becoming and being, appearance and reality. Man belongs to both worlds by virtue of the fact that he is both body and soul or mind. "God" can be known only by the control of the bodily appetites, that the mind may be free from material pollutions to contemplate the divine realities. Finally, the soul must escape from the wheel of bodily existence to return to the divine world where it really belongs.

The Hebrew view is not a dualism of two worlds, but a religious dualism of God versus man. Man is God's creature; creation is the realm of God's constant activity; and God makes himself known and speaks to men in the ebb and flow of history. Man is not a bipartite creature of the divine and human, of soul and body; in his total being he is God's creature and remains a part of creation. Therefore the redemption of man and the redemption of creation belong together. Salvation consists of fellowship with God in the midst of earthly existence and will

[111] *Ibid.*, p. 181.

[112] Josephus *War* ii. 156; Enoch 9:3, 10; Wis. 15:8, 14; IV Macc. 18:24.

[113] See Enoch 91:16; 103:4; 104:2; Jub. 23:31; IV Macc. 18:23; Wis. Sol. 3:4.

finally mean the redemption of the whole man together with his environment. At the heart of the Old Testament view is God—a living personal being—who visits man in earthly existence to establish fellowship with himself and who will finally visit man to establish his perfect rule and redemption in the world.

In sum, the Greek view is that "God" can be known only by the flight of the soul from the world and history; the Hebrew view is that God can be known because he invades history to meet men in historical experience.

Chapter Two

The Synoptic Pattern:
The Kingdom of God

Our thesis is that the unity of New Testament theology is found in the fact that the several strata share a common view of God, who visits man in history to effect the salvation of both man, the world, and history; and that diversity exists in the several interpretations of this one redemptive event. In all of the strata of the New Testament this redemptive event is both historical and eschatological in character, and stands in sharp contrast to the Greek dualistic view of man and the world.

The theological presuppositions of the Synoptic Gospels are basically those of the prophets. God is the living God, who does not stand over against the world but is its creator and sustainer. The world is not evil, nor is it the realm of evil; it is good, for it is God's creation. God cares for the least part of his creation and sustains it (Matt. 6:30).

The natural pleasures of life are gifts of God and are meant to be enjoyed. This is proved by the fact that Jesus frequently used the common illustration of a feast or banquet to describe the eschatological consummation of the Kingdom of God. The divine joy over the salvation of one lost is described in terms of feasting, merry-making, and dancing (Luke 15:23, 25). Jesus' own conduct was such that he opened himself to the charge of being a drunkard and a glutton (Matt. 11:19). In his own view, his frequent eating and drinking with tax collectors and sinners was itself a foretaste of the fellowship of the consummated Kingdom of God.

41

Furthermore, the anthropology of the Synoptic Gospels is basically that of the Old Testament, as developed in Judaism. It is the Hebrew view of man as a dynamic unity and not the Greek dualism of soul versus body. The soul (*psychē*) is the life of the body (Mark 3:4), the total living person (Mark 10:45). This is most vividly illustrated when it is used interchangeably with body (*sōma*, Matt. 6:25-26).

However, *psychē* can be used of the true center of life, designating something more than the body. The contrast between gaining the whole world or losing one's *psychē* (Mark 8:36) points to something more than physical life; it reflects the idea that the person is more than bodily existence. This is even clearer when Jesus distinguishes between the life of the body and the life of the soul and warns of the danger of a death of the soul in Gehenna (Matt. 10:28). Thus the soul is a separate entity that can exist apart from the body; but this only reflects the Jewish development of Old Testament usage. Whether or not this development is the result of Greek influence, the anthropology remains in the biblical tradition; it is quite different from Greek immortality. The few references in the Synoptics to the ultimate destiny of man do not imply a flight from the world to another realm but to the resurrection of the body (Mark 12:25; Luke 14:14).[1] The consummated Kingdom of God is viewed as occurring on earth (Matt. 25:31ff.).

The world is never viewed as evil *per se*. The world can *become* an evil thing when it comes between man and God. The gain of the whole world can mean the loss of true life (Mark 8:36); however, this is not because the world is evil, but because it becomes the object of a man's affection. This was the sin of the rich young ruler: not the fact that he was rich, but

---

[1] That the resurrected will be "like angels in heaven" is not to be understood as a reference to a heavenly destiny of God's people. The entire context assumes the Jewish doctrine of bodily resurrection on earth. Jesus' thought is that the life of the resurrection will be a very different life than present existence. Luke explains it to mean bodily immortality (Luke 20:36).

that he chose the world's riches over the Kingdom of God (Mark 10:22ff.).

That the world is in darkness (Matt. 5:14) illustrates the biblical dualism in contrast to the Greek dualism. The world is not darkness because it is the world of matter in contrast to an extra-worldly realm of light and life. The "world" here is not the sphere of nature and bodily existence; it is the world of men, of human society. The dualism is ethical and religious, not cosmological. God does not stand over against the world as mind-soul stands over against matter in two separate cosmic realms. Rather, God stands over against man because man is sinful. Salvation results not from the mastery of the body by the mind but from the devotion and obedience of heart and will to God.

The ethical character of this dualism is further illustrated by the two-age structure of the Synoptic Gospels.[2] This age is the time of evil; the age to come will be the time of the consummated Kingdom of God. However, the evil character of this age does not result from anything intrinsic in its cosmological structure; indeed, the dualism in question is eschatological and ethical, not cosmological. The two ages are two periods of time divided by the Parousia. After the dust from James Barr's assault on this citadel of Cullmann's *Heilsgeschichte* has begun to settle,[3] it still stands that in the New Testament, *houtos ho aiōn* and *ekeinos ho aiōn* designate two consecutive periods of time: the present time extending to the Parousia, and the unlimited time beyond the Parousia. Barr does prove that *aiōn* can mean both time and timelessness, that is, timeless eternity. Any reader of Kittel's *Wörterbuch* has discerned that, even if he has never read Plato. But Barr has not proved that *aiōn* in the New Testament does mean a timeless eternity.

It is of course theoretically possible that when the New Testament speaks of *houtos ho aiōn* and *ekeinos ho aiōn*, it has two different concepts in mind: this age is within created time,

---

[2] For references and critical problems, see the present author's *Jesus and the Kingdom* (1964), pp. 110ff.

[3] Cf. James Barr, *Biblical Words for Time* (1962).

and the age to come is beyond time, in timeless eternity. Sasse in his article on *kosmos* in Kittel's *Wörterbuch* does interpret the expression, *hē sunteleia tou kosmou* to mean the end of time.[4] In his article on *aiōn* (age), he speaks of the biblical doctrine of time and eternity.[5] We can agree with him that the life of the age to come is "something inconceivable, to be represented only symbolically"; we have, in fact, presented a rather detailed argument for the "semi-poetical" character of the language used to describe the world to come.[6] In spite of this fact, the biblical hope is always an earthly hope, even though its form is so inconceivable that it cannot be literally described. If the future life is in space, it is also in time. It would place an unbearable exegetical strain on the parallel expressions, *houtos ho aiōn* and *ekeinos ho aiōn*, to understand the first to mean time and the second something quite different, such as a timeless eternity. At this point, Cullmann is certainly right; both words designate contiguous periods of time.

Historically speaking, the idea of the future *aiōn* derives directly from the Old Testament and stands in contrast with Greek thinking. God, who acts in the present in history, will yet act decisively in the (near) future to establish his perfect reign. The result will be a blessed existence on a redeemed earth with infinitely prolonged existence (Isa. 65:20) or even immortal life (Isa. 25:8). In Judaism and the New Testament the same pattern of redemption remains—present evil, future bliss—with a mighty visitation of God dividing the two eras. The idiom of this age and the age to come is the descriptive terminology for these two eras. This way of thinking stands in complete contrast to the Greek dualism of time versus eternity, for the latter depends on its phenomenal-noumenal dualism, which is cosmological and not eschatological in character. The phenomenal is the realm of becoming, change, flux, of time; the noumenal is the realm of being, permanence, stability, of eternity.

---

[4] H. Sasse, *TDNT*, III, 885.
[5] *Ibid.*, I, 205.
[6] *Jesus and the Kingdom*, pp. 43ff., 58ff., 312.

The fundamental biblical difference between the two ages is not one of matter versus spirit, or phenomena versus noumena, or visible versus invisible realities. The difference is between sin versus righteousness and mortality versus immortality.[7] This age is evil because of its cares and delights and desires which turn the hearts of men away from God (Mark 4:18ff.). It is the era of death because men have been turned away from God by the love of the things of the world (Mark 10:23ff., 30). The enjoyment of the things of the world is not itself evil; when they become an object of affection instead of the rule of God, they become sinful. The sin is in the affections and hearts of men, not in the world itself. The blessings of the future age are, to be sure, as yet invisible; but they will become visible at the Parousia.

If, then, the theology of the Synoptic Gospels is not a theology of escape of the souls of men from this world to another world, it can be positively described as a theology of God's invasion into the world and history. We have seen that the Old Testament theology has at its center the idea of "God who comes," who visits his people, who meets them for blessing and judgment in the midst of earthly historical experience. The central theme of the theology of the Synoptic Gospels is that the God who visited Israel in Egypt to deliver them, to make them his people, who visited them again and again in the events of their historical experience, who constantly held before them the promise of a final eschatological[8] hour, when he would visit Israel to consummate his redemptive purpose, has now acted in Jesus of Nazareth to fulfill this promise. Here is the essential link between the Old and New Testaments: redemptive history. "The chief considerations in the correspondence between the

[7] There are numerous sayings in the New Testament, such as II Cor. 4:18, that taken out of context would seem to offer a flat refutation of this statement. But see the following chapters.

[8] For the technical definition of "eschatology" as applied to the Old Testament promises, see *Jesus and the Kingdom*. Basically the same position is expressed by G. von Rad, *Old Testament Theology* (1965), II, 114ff.

two testaments does not lie primarily in the field of religious terminology, but in that of saving history, for in Jesus Christ we meet once again—and in a more intensified form—with the same inter-connection between divine word and historical acts with which we are already so familiar in the Old Testament."[9]

This comment by Professor von Rad recognizes the two important facts about both the Old and New Testaments: they are both the recital of historical events and the record of interpreting words that bring out the meaning of events. This accounts for the character of the Gospels as both report and witness. Many form critics have felt that because the Gospels are written by men of faith who not only report events in history but also witness to their faith in the meaning of these events, the Gospels cannot be trustworthy historical records, but that faith must have distorted the historical facts. However, this view is not a necessary conclusion drawn from objective unprejudiced scientific study; on the contrary, it rests upon certain presuppositions of what "history" must be like. "History" cannot be the scene of objective visible acts of God. "History" has no room for such a person as Jesus Christ as he is pictured in the Gospels. "History" cannot tolerate the idea of an actual resurrection from the dead. Since such facts as these constitute the substance of the Gospels, they cannot be taken as historical, but must be seen as confessions of faith in mythological form. This so-called "scientific" understanding of history, which dominates much contemporary New Testament study, decides in advance the limits of what could and could not have happened and is compelled by its own presuppositions to downgrade seriously the reliability of the Gospels. Carl Braaten has recently issued the call for a new concept of history, "freed from a mechanistic and pessimistic definition of the nature of history,"[10] and able to handle more adequately the New Testament witness.

The Gospels are a record of the historical event of Jesus Christ, whose revelational and redemptive meaning is interpreted

[9] G. von Rad, *op. cit.*, II, 382.
[10] Carl Braaten, *History and Hermeneutics* (1966), p. 100.

first by the words of Jesus himself, and further by the prophetic-apostolic witness of the church. It is arbitrary and foreign to the biblical perspective to separate kerygma—believing proclamation of the early church—and trustworthy factual report, as many contemporary scholars have done.[11] A neutral, uncommitted, "objective" observer could not write a gospel, for a gospel is good news of what God has done in history (Mark 1:14). The Synoptic Gospels share a common theme: that the time promised by the Old Testament prophets is fulfilled, that God is visiting his people in the person of Jesus Christ for their salvation (Mark 1:15; Luke 4:21; Matt. 4:14ff.).

The central theme of the Synoptic Gospels is the Kingdom of God. This is a theme that has particularly concerned the author through the years, because it is clearly the center of the Lord's teaching, and because in undergraduate days of theological study, no available interpretation of the Kingdom of God seemed to square with the biblical data. Here was an amazing fact: the central theme of the Lord's message was obscured by the confusing diversity of modern interpretations. For this reason, the study of the Kingdom of God has become a central concern and has occupied his study.

The central problem confronting the modern understanding of the Kingdom of God is its relationship to history in view of the so-called modern man's understanding of history. The major options may be briefly summarized.[12]

[11] J. M. Robinson, *The New Quest of the Historical Jesus* (1959), p. 37.

[12] For a full survey, see *Jesus and the Kingdom*, pp. 3-40; for detailed histories of interpretation, see Norman Perrin, *The Kingdom of God in the Teaching of Jesus* (1963), and G. Lundström, *The Kingdom of God in the Teaching of Jesus* (1963). Both of these books embody doctoral dissertations, and both are, strictly speaking, improperly named, for they are not comprehensive studies of the teaching of Jesus, but surveys of history of interpretation of Jesus' teaching about the Kingdom of God. Lundström throws his net somewhat wider than Perrin, including a number of theologians as well as exegetes. Perrin's book is at places more accurate than Lundström's. Perrin has given us a thoroughly competent, well-written, stimulating book, which is strongly to be recommended as a history of interpretation of this theme.

The idealist view of old liberalism viewed the Kingdom of God in quite unhistorical terms as a set of timeless religious and spiritual values that have to do with the soul and God. The Kingdom affects history only as men in history accept the standards of the Kingdom and thus influence history.

A modern variant of this is the Realized Eschatology of C. H. Dodd. The eschatological language by which the Kingdom is described in the Gospels is, according to Dodd, only a symbolic way of referring to the transcendental order that is beyond time and space. Jesus employed the traditional symbolism of apocalyptic to indicate the other-worldly or absolute character of the Kingdom of God.[13] In the ministry of Jesus, the timeless, the eternal, the transcendental has entered history.[14] Apart from the Greek form of the language, this sounds as though the Kingdom of God was actually concerned with history. However, this is not, in reality, the case, for the consummation of the Kingdom will not occur in history but in this transcendent order beyond time and space. This appears to mean that the Kingdom has to do with personal immortality, not with the destiny of human history.[15] Perrin has correctly criticized this as being a thoroughly unbiblical view;[16] he is right in insisting that the eschatological consummation both in the Old Testament and New Testament, and (usually) in Judaism, occurs on the earth. Dodd's Realized Eschatology, therefore, is

---

13 C. H. Dodd, *The Parables of the Kingdom* (1936), pp. 56, 197.
14 *Ibid.*, pp. 107f.
15 See C. H. Dodd, *The Coming of Christ* (1951), p. 26: "When each individual person reaches the frontier post he steps into the presence of the Eternal. And when, in due course, history ends, and the *human race perishes from this planet*, it will encounter God" (italics mine).
16 *Op. cit.*, pp. 69-72. Perrin bases his criticism of Dodd on the premise that Judaism knows nothing of a salvation that is consummated in the heavenly realm. Such an idea does, however, appear in Enoch 91:16, which is not a re-creation of heaven and earth (*op. cit.*, p. 166), but only of the heaven. In Enoch 104:2, Jubilees 23:31, and Enoch 103:4, there is a future life of the spirit without bodily resurrection. However, the beliefs of Judaism must not be allowed to determine what Jesus could or could not have thought, and Perrin's criticism of Dodd is valid in spite of this careless statement.

not really concerned with history, and it is not clear how in Dodd's thought the Kingdom affects history.

Consistent Eschatology represents Jesus' teaching as being concerned only with the end of history, not with its present. The Kingdom of God is exclusively the apocalyptic act of God breaking into history in the very near future; it has no relationship to history until it will bring history to its apocalyptic end. However, for the classical defenders of Consistent Eschatology, this view has no relevance for the modern man or for any permanent doctrine of the Kingdom of God, for Jesus was a deluded Jewish apocalyptist who proclaimed an apocalyptic event that did not happen and which the "modern man" does not believe ever can happen. This is what Schweitzer meant by saying that the historical Jesus cannot be a help but only an offense to modern religion. The deluded Jewish apocalyptist[17] remains a stranger to our time.[18]

The existential eschatology of Bultmann accepts the Consistent Eschatology of J. Weiss and A. Schweitzer and does not hide the fact that the eschatological teaching of Jesus is not palatable for modern man. Any realistic ideas about an apocalyptic act of God transforming the world and human history so that a new earth becomes the scene of a redeemed people is fantastic and offensive to intelligence; it is a *sacrificium intellectus*. The only possible way for our world to come to its end is by natural catastrophe, not by the mythical idea found in the New Testament of an apocalyptic act of God.[19]

However, Bultmann does not, like Schweitzer, turn away from Jesus' proclamation of the Kingdom to some other philosophy—in Schweitzer's case, reverence for life—for his own religion. He "demythologizes" Jesus' message of the apocalyptic Kingdom. That is, he interprets it in terms of human existence. The Kingdom of God *means* the sovereignty of God, the abso-

---

[17] This is not Schweitzer's phrase, but it expresses his understanding of Jesus.

[18] A. Schweitzer, *The Quest of the Historical Jesus* (1911), p. 399.

[19] R. Bultmann, *Kerygma and Myth* (1953), I, 5.

luteness of his will for human existence, and has nothing to say about the goal of history or human destiny. Jesus' apocalyptic proclamation was only the reflex of his overwhelming conscious-ness of God. "The essential thing about the eschatological mes-sage is the idea of God that operates in it and the idea of human existence—not the belief that the end of the world is just ahead."[20] Thus the Kingdom of God has no real relevance for history, only for my individual historicity. In fact, says Bult-mann, "Today we cannot claim to know the end and the goal of history. Therefore the question of meaning in history has become meaningless."[21] Bultmann bolsters his program of de-mythologizing by insisting that the real *intent* of the New Testa-ment is to say something about human existence, not about human history. The form of expression, namely, that God will act in history in an apocalyptic event to transform the world and establish his Kingdom, is only the mythological form of this existential understanding. Therefore, Bultmann insists he is utterly loyal to the gospel when he discards the first-century mythological form and preserves its existential intent. Here is where the debate must first be carried out. What is the *intent* of the New Testament?

While the apocalyptic nature of the coming of the Kingdom as understood by Consistent Eschatology has been very widely accepted as the historical form of Jesus' teaching, a number of scholars have modified the consistent futurity of the Kingdom to recognize both a present and a future aspect. This has been done in various ways. Kümmel sees the imminent apocalyptic Kingdom present in the person of Jesus. Cullmann sees two days in the divine war with evil: D-day occurred at the midpoint of history in Jesus Christ when the powers of evil were broken by the Kingdom of God; V-day will be the day of the Parousia when the Kingdom will destroy the powers of evil and will fill the world. Other scholars have suggested the formula: promise of the Kingdom (in the Old Testament), fulfillment of the

[20] R. Bultmann, *Theology of the New Testament* (1951), I, 23.
[21] R. Bultmann, *History and Eschatology* (1957), p. 120.

Kingdom (in Jesus' ministry), consummation of the Kingdom (at the Parousia).[22] However, for many of these scholars, the problem of any sort of realistic eschatology remains a difficult problem. How *can* an intelligent modern man take seriously the apocalyptic forecasts of the New Testament?[23] Nevertheless, for these interpreters, the Kingdom is concerned with history. It has broken into history in Jesus Christ, and it will involve a consummation in power either in history or at the end of history.

The present author has the conviction that this last view is correct, but with modifications. We shall offer here a brief summary of the view expounded in detail in *Jesus and the Kingdom* in the light of the contemporary discussion. The truth of the Kingdom of God is rooted in the prophetic view of God who comes to his people in history, who reveals his redemptive and judicial purpose in historical events. The Old Testament sees God acting in the sequence of events in Israel's history, and it continually looks forward to a final, decisive act in history to establish his Kingdom. The new redeemed order is described in different ways, but there are four constants: it results from a visitation of God, a divine inbreaking; this occurs in history, not in personal individual experience; the new order stands in continuity with the old order, in that it is always viewed as earthly existence; yet there is also discontinuity in that the new order involves a transformation of the old and the emergence of something that has never existed before.

As to the question of the time of the coming of the Kingdom, the Hebrews did not have an abstract idea of time or eternity. All that Israel knew was time containing events. The question of whether the consummation takes place in time or in eternity is foreign to the Old Testament.[24] Time is simply the setting in which events occur, in this instance, in which God acts. The important thing is not time but the events that fill it.

[22] A. M. Hunter, R. Schnackenburg.
[23] See our criticism of W. G. Kümmel in *Jesus and the Kingdom* (1964), pp. 29, 309f.
[24] G. von Rad, *Old Testament Theology* (1965), II, 100, 114.

Since it is God who acts—God who is the eternal one[25]—his present acts in history and his final act consummating redemption can be viewed as though they were a single act; for it is one God who is acting in the present and who will act in the indeterminate future for the one redemptive purpose that fills the prophetic consciousness. The dynamic tension between history and eschatology stands at the heart of the prophetic perspective.

The prophetic eschatology was developed in Judaism, and the contrast between the present order and the future so sharpened that a dualistic terminology of this age and the age to come emerged. This idiom is not found in the Old Testament but occurs in both first-century Judaism and the New Testament. We have argued that this does not result from the assimilation of Persian or Babylonian ideas, whatever that influence may have been, but is a legitimate development of the Old Testament theology of the Kingdom coming by rupture, that is, divine visitation. In other words, the prophetic view of history is at this central point essentially apocalyptic. We cannot support the position of many scholars that the prophetic view sees a Kingdom arising from within history while the apocalyptic view envisions a Kingdom breaking into history. The prophetic eschatology embodies a divine act, a theophany.

Among the differences between prophetic and apocalyptic, the most notable is the apocalyptic loss of the sense of God's acting in present history. The prophetic tension between the present and future, between history and eschatology, is lost. God is no longer working redemptively in the present. This age is given over to evil. God's people can expect only suffering and affliction from the enemies of God, both human and superhuman, until the end of the age. This age is irreparably evil. But God is still God, although for the present his withdrawal and inactivity presents an insoluble problem of theodicy for God's righteous people. However, at the time decreed, which is always

[25] See W. Eichrodt, *Theology of the Old Testament* (1961), I, 182f.

52

viewed as being in the near future, God will act; his Kingdom will be gloriously established in all the earth.

The key to Jesus' proclamation of the Kingdom of God is found in the dynamic understanding of that term. God's Kingdom is first of all his kingly rule, his sovereign redeeming activity, and secondarily the realm of blessing inaugurated by the divine act. The proclamation of the coming of the Kingdom of God is the announcement, as in Judaism, of the inbreaking of God into human history to establish his will. At this point, Jesus' message is apocalyptic. He heralds a divine visitation that will end this age and inaugurate the age to come.

We have argued that this apocalyptic act will be a real event that will effect a transformation of the present order; but we have tried to establish that both the prophets and Jesus described this future event and the ensuing order in "semipoetical" language. By this we mean to say that both the divine visitation and the new order, while standing in continuity with the present order, will be so different from all human experience as to be truly ineffable. There are no terms of present experience that can accurately describe it; therefore, picturesque, symbolic language must be used. It is, however, not *merely* poetical, that is, symbolic language used to describe concepts of "spiritual," other-worldly realities. We call it "semipoetical"; for while the language is poetical, it designates real future events of cosmic proportions, indescribable though they be. This apocalyptic event of the coming of the Kingdom and the transformation of the present order is the consummation of the entire Old Testament prophetic hope in all of its diversity.

If some scholars speak of this view as being a Kingdom "beyond history"—language that we are willing to accept—it should not be interpreted to mean an order beyond time and space, in eternity or heaven rather than on this earth, but only that the new order of a redeemed earth and a transformed society will be so different from present human historical experience that it can be described only as being "beyond history." "Historical" existence in this instance is not synonymous with earthly existence. Rather, it means earthly existence *as we now know it*. The scene of the eschatological is always a new earth in biblical thought, and usually such in Jewish apocalyptic. Even in apocalyptic, there is envisaged the continuation of time and history after the historical consummation.[26] However, because of the modern debate, even though it is a nonbiblical way of thinking, we may use the term "beyond history" to describe the new order that will witness the transformation of the structure of present history; and we may use the term "the end of history" to designate the end of the present order as we know it.

This apocalyptic hope of the Gospels is essentially one with the hopes of both apocalyptic and rabbinic Judaism of a divine visitation to establish the Kingdom of God.[27] There is in Jesus' proclamation, however, a distinctive, novel, unique element that finds no parallel in Judaism, namely, that before the apocalyptic consummation at the end of history, a fulfillment of the prophetic hope has occurred within history; that before the coming of God's Kingdom as a cosmic event, his Kingdom has come as an event in history; that before God acts as King to inaugurate the redeemed order, he has acted in Jesus of Nazareth to bring to men in advance of the eschatological consummation the blessings of actual fulfillment. The Old Testament *promise* of the coming of the Kingdom, *fulfillment* of the promise of the Kingdom in history in the person, words, and deeds of Jesus, *consummation* of the promise at the end of history—this is the basic structure of the theology of the Synoptic Gospels.

Here is the unique element in Jesus' teaching, and Dodd is right in stressing its centrality and distinctiveness.[28] There is to be sure something analogous in rabbinic Judaism, which saw the Kingdom as God's kingly rule available to men in the present in the divinely given law. Men may take upon themselves the yoke of the Kingdom by accepting the law as their

26 G. von Rad, *op. cit.*, II, 114. See Perrin's denial of a transcendental eschatology, *op. cit.*, p. 71.

27 See J. Klausner, *The Messianic Hope in Israel* (1955), part III, for the view of rabbinic Judaism. See footnote on p. 25.

28 *The Parables of the Kingdom* (1936), p. 49.

54

rule of life. However, God's Kingdom does not *come*; it is there in the law; God is in heaven.

When Jesus proclaimed that the Kingdom *has come* (Matt. 12:28) in his own person and mission, he proclaimed something new and unheard of in Judaism. This is the "mystery" of the Kingdom (Mark 4:11): the revelation of a new redemptive act—that before the eschatological theophany, God has invaded history to bring men the blessings of his redemptive reign.

This coming of the Kingdom is a real event in history. Jesus spoke, and his words embodied the power of the Kingdom. He acted, and his deeds were the working of the Kingdom. They are objective historical events: words, deeds, and relationships created by the coming of the Kingdom in Jesus.

Yet while this event could be seen by all, it was not universally understood. All men saw the deeds of the Kingdom, but some understood them to be the deeds of the devil (Matt. 12:24). All men heard Jesus' words, but instead of the Kingdom of God, some saw insanity (Mark 3:21). The deeds could be seen, the words heard, the person of Jesus encountered; but the form of the presence of the Kingdom in him was such that it required a human response to be recognized for what it was. Only the spiritually responsive could understand Jesus' teaching and see in his mission the coming of the Kingdom (Matt. 13:10-17). Only those with childlike faith had eyes to see and ears to hear; the wise and understanding were blind and deaf (Matt. 11:25ff.).

This is why some scholars speak of the presence of the Kingdom in Jesus in a "hidden" or "veiled" form. Jesus, his words, and his deeds were public events open to all, and the significance of these events was proclaimed to all. But the presence of the Kingdom was "hidden," not only because it had come in an utterly unexpected way, but because it was manifested in historical acts and words that could be differently understood. The deeds were completely meaningful only when accompanied by words. The words interpreted the deeds; but to the spiritually blind it was nonsense, not the Kingdom of God.

55

The proclamation of the Kingdom means a twofold event, or two acts in a single divine redemption: a visitation in history hidden in the person of Jesus, and a visitation at the end of history in an unveiled cosmic event. How these two are related temporarily is one of the most difficult questions to decide, because of their nature. Both the historical and the eschatological are acts of God: visitations of the God of heaven to men on earth, for the same end—the establishing of God's rule on earth.

In the Gospels there is the same prophetic tension between history and eschatology that appears in the prophets but was lost in the apocalyptists. The same God who will act at the end of history is acting in history for the same purpose: to establish his reign on earth among men. The question of chronology is altogether secondary to the fact. Sometimes a distinction is made between the present and the future; sometimes the future looms up and dominates the present, as in the Old Testament. Our analytical way of thinking destroys something very important in the biblical perspective—an inescapable dynamic tension between the present and future.

The structure of the theology of the Kingdom of God contrasts sharply with the Greek soul-body, earth-heaven dualism, where salvation means escape from bodily life in this world to the other world of God. The Kingdom of God means the coming of God in Jesus Christ into history to bring his rule to men. It embodies a twofold dualism: the coming of the God of heaven to men on earth and the present expectation of the future establishment of the Kingdom on the earth.

It is not altogether accurate to describe the dualism of the Synoptic Gospels as a simple eschatological dualism of the present and the future. This dualism itself rests on another dualism: that of God versus man. This is not like the Greek cosmological dualism, but is religious and ethical. God is the creator; man is made in the image of God, but is a disobedient sinner. Therefore the God of heaven visits man in history to accomplish his salvation, which will be consummated in time and space on earth.

56

For this reason, heaven is a significant biblical concept, not as the destiny of the redeemed, but as the dwelling place of God. Although there is no difference in meaning between the terms "Kingdom of God" and "Kingdom of the heavens," the latter reminds us that God does not dwell on earth but in heaven. In effect, the coming of the Kingdom means the coming of heaven to earth, so that finally in the consummation earth and its redeemed society share the blessings of heaven—righteousness, peace, immortality.

Thus the Gospels can speak of heaven as a present reality without importing anything from Greek dualism. Men are exhorted to lay up treasure in heaven, for where one's treasure is, there will his heart be (Matt. 6:20). The faithful can be said to have a reward in the heavens (Matt. 5:12). The rich young ruler is told that if he will meet the demands of discipleship, he will have treasure in heaven and will inherit eternal life in the Kingdom of God in the age to come (Mark 11:21, 30). Such sayings do not mean that the promised blessings are destined to be enjoyed in heaven; salvation will be accomplished in the age to come on a transformed earth when the God of heaven comes to dwell among his people on earth,[29] bringing to the redeemed the life and blessings of heaven.

The theology of the Kingdom of God is a theology of the invasion of history by the God of heaven in the person of Jesus of Nazareth to bring history to its consummation in the age to come beyond history. And the age to come may be spoken of as "beyond history" because heaven has invaded history and raised it to a higher level in a new redeemed order.

Any worthy theology must sustain itself by dialogue with other theologies. Therefore, in concluding this chapter, we would undertake a comparison of the theology of the Kingdom here summarized with that defended in a book which appeared after the present author had completed his own study of the

---

[29] This idea, explicit in Rev. 21:22, is implicit in many of the metaphors of the Gospels. See J. Jeremias, *The Parables of Jesus* (1963), pp. 222f.

Kingdom of God, Norman Perrin's *The Kingdom of God in the Teaching of Jesus.*[30] This comparison is of particular interest to the author because Perrin has written a major review of the author's *Jesus and the Kingdom* and has nothing but severely negative judgments about the merit of the work in question and the quality of its workmanship. Perrin thinks that the author has an uncritical view of the Gospels, a curious methodology, and a one-sided approach to the question of authenticity. He accuses him of misunderstanding other contemporary scholars, of dismissing contemptuously what he does not agree with, and standing "with his face turned resolutely upstream, whence we all came some considerable time ago."[31] An analysis of the points where Perrin agrees or disagrees with the present author therefore should be enlightening.

Perrin's position and that of the present author are, surprisingly, very close, although Perrin's conclusions are based more on interaction with the history of criticism than with exegetical data. In the following we shall outline the important elements in Perrin's view that are similar to those of the present author.

Dalman was right in insisting that the basic meaning of the Kingdom of God is the reign, the kingly activity of God,[32] even though he emphasized the rabbinic at the expense of the apocalyptic view of the divine inbreaking. In Judaism, the meaning of the Kingdom of God is twofold: "God's decisive intervention in history and human experience, and the final state of the redeemed to which that intervention leads." In other words, the Kingdom is God's kingly rule[33] manifested to create a realm of blessing for men. Perrin emphasizes constantly that history is the scene of God's activity.[34] He distinguishes, as does the present author, between the prophetic view, which sees God active in historical events, and the apocalyptic view, which sees

[30] Philadelphia: Westminster, 1963.
[31] Norman Perrin, "Against the Current," *Interpretation,* XIX (1965), 228-231.
[32] Perrin, *The Kingdom of God in the Teaching of Jesus,* p. 27.
[33] *Ibid.,* p. 167.
[34] *Ibid.,* pp. 161ff.

history as a vast predetermined movement; and he insists, rightly, that Jesus held to the prophetic view and rejected the apocalyptic.[35] He insists strongly on the nature of the Jewish and biblical hope as being on the earth in time, and he rejects modernizing, transcendentalizing interpretations such as that of C. H. Dodd.[36]

Coming to the message of Jesus, Perrin holds, as does the present author, that Jesus' proclamation of the Kingdom is an apocalyptic event.[37] To this extent, Weiss and Schweitzer were right. However, Dodd was also right in recognizing the Kingdom as really present in Jesus' mission. Perrin rejects efforts such as that of R. H. Fuller to translate the presence of the Kingdom into a proleptic present or nearness. The Kingdom is really present.[38]

The relationship between present and future Perrin finds to be that of present event in Jesus and future consummation of what was begun in that event. This is the central thesis of *Jesus*

[35] *Ibid.*, p. 164. Perrin does not emphasize the apocalyptic loss of God's acting in history in the way the present author has done, nor does he discuss the frequent critical bifurcation between apocalyptic and prophetic eschatologies in such scholars as Goguel, Waterman, and J. W. Bowman. He fails to deal with a suggestion made by the present author some time ago that it might be better to distinguish between prophetic-apocalyptic and non-prophetic-apocalyptic ("Why not Prophetic-Apocalyptic?", *JBL*, LXXVI [1957], 192-200). This leads Perrin to distinguish between prophetic and apocalyptic, and at the same time to speak of the prophetic-apocalyptic view (pp. 27, 59, 60). Yet despite these differences, his basic thought structure is the same as that of *Jesus and the Kingdom*.

[36] *Ibid.*, pp. 67, 73, 86.

[37] Perrin's effort, according to the rules of advanced form criticism, to find something distinctive (and therefore authentic) in the eschatological teaching of Jesus in contrast to Jewish thought appears to the present author to be special pleading. When Jesus spoke of the "coming" of the eschatological Kingdom and the Jews spoke of the "appearing" or "establishing" of the Kingdom, they are saying the same thing even though they use different words (Perrin, *Recovering the Teaching of Jesus* [1967], pp. 58ff.). If one applied consistently the rules of form criticism, namely, that all alleged sayings of Jesus that have parallels either in Judaism or in early Christianity cannot be trusted, it is difficult to see how one can attribute sayings about an eschatological Kingdom to Jesus, as do the Bultmannians.

[38] *Ibid.*, p. 87.

and the Kingdom. One of the most frequent emphases of Perrin's book is that the future means consummation of what was begun in Jesus' ministry.[39] There is thus an inescapable tension between present and future.[40] The nature of the future consummation is such that it cannot be described factually. Eschatological language is therefore pictorial, and cannot be interpreted literally.[41]

Perrin's understanding of the Kingdom of God in the teaching of Jesus and that of the present author are basically the same. There are, however, two positions that are essential to Perrin's position with which we cannot agree, because they do not square with the biblical data. These two positions reflect Perrin's effort as a "modern man" to demythologize the eschatology of the Kingdom of God. First, he confuses the historical and the eschatological visitations of the Kingdom. He rightly insists that the Kingdom is present in Jesus' mission and awaits a future consummation; but when he discusses the Kingdom as God's decisive intervention in history, he finds this decisive intervention,[42] which in Judaism was an apocalyptic event, to be taught by Jesus in such passages as Matthew 12:28; 11:12f. and Luke 17:20. Here is a flaw that weakens Perrin's entire structure. These passages do not refer to the apocalyptic event, but to that element in Jesus' teaching which has no analogy in Judaism. Rabbinic Judaism saw the rule of God as present among men in obedience to the law; but this is not a *coming* of the Kingdom. The Kingdom is present among men in the law; it will *come* at the end of the age. Jesus' message proclaimed something new, namely, that in his person, deeds, and words God had unexpectedly visited men in history before the decisive apocalyptic event. This is the "mystery" of the Kingdom, the new revelation of God's kingly rule—a concept that Perrin does not discuss.

Secondly, Perrin appears to speak in a self-contradictory way

---

[39] *Ibid.*, pp. 86, 139, 140, 145, 188, 189, 190, 198, 199.
[40] *Ibid.*, pp. 135, 159.
[41] *Ibid.*, p. 85.
[42] *Ibid.*, pp. 168ff.

when he insists that "Jesus' use of the phrase is consistent, and wholly in accord with its use in apocalyptic,"[43] and yet recognizes that the Kingdom was actually present in history in Jesus of Nazareth, while its consummation would occur in the future. *Such an idea of a coming of the Kingdom in history is foreign to Jewish apocalyptic*; but it is the heart of Jesus' message. At this central point Jesus' teaching is not consistent with Jewish apocalyptic. This is why the presence of the Kingdom can be spoken of as "hidden," as Perrin admits.[44] The decisive intervention of God will not be hidden. "Jesus expected in the future an event which would mark the end of the existing order of things and bring to consummation that which had begun in his own ministry."[45] When Perrin speaks as clearly as this about the future, and yet sees in Jesus' mission the decisive event that he claims is thoroughly consistent with apocalyptic, he only confuses his readers.

If the event in history is the decisive intervention of God, how does Perrin conceive of the consummation? All we can say is that he does not know, nor do his readers know what he is thinking. Here again, he appears to be inconsistent. On the one hand, he argues that Jesus expected the end of the existing order of events in the future consummation.[46] But when he tries to interpret the *meaning* of this consummation, he writes:

> We may not therefore resolve the tension between present and future for us as individuals by externalizing the future teaching in terms of cosmic catastrophe and the descent of a heavenly being, nor may we refer it to a heavenly realm or to a life beyond death. There is no warrant for any of this in the teaching of Jesus. To do justice to this teaching we must hold fast to the conviction that the consummation

---

[43] *Ibid.*, p. 153. If this is so, according to Perrin's understanding of form criticism, such sayings of Jesus should not be considered authentic, see above, p. 82.

[44] *Ibid.*, p. 139.

[45] *Ibid.*, p. 140.

[46] *Ibid.*, pp. 140, 156, 157.

of that which has begun in the ministry of Jesus *will be,* and that it will be just as much a reality to be experienced as was the beginning in the ministry of Jesus and in the experience of those who first believed in him. How? When? Where? may be natural questions but they are illegitimate questions in view of the fact that the teaching of Jesus seems deliberately to avoid anything that could be construed as an answer to them. . . . This teaching puts the emphasis where it belongs: on the state of tension between the present and future in which the believer must live and move and have his being.[47]

The key words in this passage are in the second line: "for us as individuals." Perrin correctly understands the contemporary hermeneutical problem in interpreting the Kingdom of God. Is it to be interpreted existentially as Bultmann and his followers do, or historically?[48] This is indeed the problem; and Perrin's choice is clear; he selects the existentialist understanding. "The common factor in all of these points [of the presence of the Kingdom in Jesus' mission] is that they are directly related to the experience of the individual." Bultmann has succeeded in showing that "the sphere of individual human existence is the sphere in which the Kingdom of God is manifested."[49] Perrin insists that Jesus explicitly rejects all externalization to concentrate on the experience of the individual. Therefore, he concludes that the consummation, though pictured in apocalyptic language, really *means* something in human experience, not in human history. "So the tension between present and future is a tension, above all, within human experience."[50]

Thus Perrin asserts that the real meaning of the Kingdom of God is existential; but he does not present a convincing proof of his position. Assertion is not demonstration. It is clear that

---

[47] *Ibid.,* p. 190.
[48] *Ibid.,* pp. 119, 123, 159.
[49] *Ibid.,* p. 186.
[50] *Ibid.,* p. 199. It is clear from Perrin's language elsewhere that "human experience" does not designate human history but personal individual experience. See p. 191.

the presence of the Kingdom in Jesus' mission has inescapable existential, that is, personal, consequences. The Kingdom of God is concerned with my existence, my personal response and responsibility, my freedom from bondage to the past, to sin, to all of this is true because first of all something happened *in* pride, to the world. It demands openness to God's future. But *history.* Jesus was a historical person. His words were historical events. His deeds involved other people; but they were far larger than the boundaries of personal existence. His deeds included interpersonal fellowship, healings of bodies as well as minds. His mission created a new fellowship of men; and this fellowship after the resurrection became the Christian church, which has become one of the most influential institutions in Western culture. All of this happened in history; and it is only because certain events first happened in history that other results were experienced in the existential dimension. Existential impact results only from historical event. Therefore, when Perrin emphasizes, as he does, and excellently, that in Jesus an event occurred in history, and then attempts to reduce the eschatological consummation to existential terms, we can only conclude that his effort has failed. I have no idea what he means by his summary statement, "The kingly activity of God . . . will continue until it reaches its climax in the consummation"[51]; I have no idea, even though I have read and reread his pages.

Our interaction with Perrin has served, we trust, to accentuate our central thesis: that the Kingdom of God is the invasion of the God of heaven into human history for the purpose of establishing his reign among men; but this invasion involves two acts: the veiled coming of the Kingdom in past history in the mission of Jesus and a glorious coming at the end of history to consummate what was begun in history; the defeat of the powers of evil, of decay and death, and the triumph of righteousness and life. The Kingdom of God means that God brings heaven to earth, and that the earth will share the heavenly life and glory.

[51] *Ibid.,* p. 199.

Chapter Three

The Johannine Pattern:
Eternal Life

Probably few scholars will disagree with our central thesis as it applies to the Synoptic Gospels, namely, that the theology of the Kingdom of God found there stands in the Hebrew-Jewish prophetic-apocalyptic tradition of a God who brings salvation to man on earth, and that it is in sharp contrast to the Greek salvation of flight from the world to a transcendental divine realm. We have, however, developed this thesis at some length so that we can have a full background for comparison with the theology of John and of Paul.

We cannot deny that the theology of John seems to be a world apart from that of the Synoptics. The Kingdom of God, which is the central message of the Synoptics, appears only three times in John (John 3:3, 5; 18:36), and then only incidentally. Its place is taken by the concept of eternal life. Eternal life does indeed appear in the Synoptic Gospels, but always as an eschatological blessing; it is the life of the age to come after the resurrection, as in Daniel 12:2 (Mark 9:43, 45; Matt. 7:14; 25:46). In John, the predominant emphasis upon eternal life is quite different. It is that of a life present among men in the person of Jesus Christ, to be received and lived here and now (John 3:36, *passim*).

Paralleling this difference between an eschatological Kingdom of God in the Synoptics and realized eternal life in John is an apparently different dualism. The Synoptic Gospels, like Judaism, emphasize the eschatological dualism of the two ages: this age of evil, and the age to come that will witness the Kingdom of God in its glorious consummation.[1] This terminology of the two ages is lacking in John; and the eschatological dualism at first appearance seems to be replaced by a cosmological dualism of two worlds: heaven and earth. One of Britain's most able Johannine scholars has expressed it this way: ". . . elsewhere in the New Testament the predominant eschatological contrast is that between the present age and the age to come—a temporal contrast—in John it is between two orders of existence, the temporal and the eternal."[2] This difference must not be glossed over in the interests of harmonizing the Gospels; the difference is real.

John constantly contrasts heaven and earth. Jesus asked Nicodemus how he could expect to understand heavenly things that have to do with the new birth and eternal life when he could not even understand common earthly things having to do with natural birth (John 3:12). Jesus belongs to this higher order of existence while men belong to the earth. "You are from below, I am from above; you are of this world, I am not of this world" (John 8:23). This is the central truth of the Gospel: that Jesus is not a mere man but has come from heaven to earth to bring men knowledge of God and eternal life. He is the light who has come into the world (3:19) and shines in the darkness of this world (1:9). He is the bread that comes down from heaven (6:33, 51; 12:46). He came from God (13:3; 16:38) in heaven (6:38), and after completing his work on earth will return to the Father in heaven (7:33; 13:1, 3; 16:5, 28). Instead of the coming of the eschatological Kingdom of God found in the Synoptics there is the coming from heaven to earth of the pre-existent Son to bring light and life in the darkness of the world.

Another striking element in the Johannine dualism is the contrast between light and darkness. "The light shines in the

---

[1] For references, see *Jesus and the Kingdom* (1964), pp. 111ff.
[2] J. N. Sanders in *Interpreter's Dictionary of the Bible*, II, 938.

darkness, and the darkness has not overcome it" (1:5). The world is the realm of darkness but God is light (I John 1:5), and Jesus came to bring light into the darkness (3:19; 12:46; 8:12). Here is the one source of true light; every man who finds light must find it in Christ (1:9).[3] This light is still shining, and the darkness has not been able to quench it (1:5). The antithesis of light and darkness is a further aspect of the Johannine dualism of above versus below, heaven versus the world, and appears to substitute a present "vertical" dualism for the Synoptic temporal, eschatological dualism.

Again, there is in John a contrast between flesh and spirit lacking in the Synoptics. "That which is born of the flesh is flesh, and that which is born of the Spirit is spirit" (3:6). "It is the spirit that gives life, the flesh is of no avail" (6:63). Such sayings suggest two orders of existence, similar to Greek dualism.

On the surface, John seems to have transformed the Jewish Synoptic dualism into a thoroughly Greek type of dualism. This has led Dodd to the conclusion that eschatology has been sublimated into a distinctive kind of mysticism. That is, instead of salvation in the eschatological Kingdom of God, John teaches that the life of eternity has been brought by Christ into the world to be experienced here and now in fellowship with him. "Its underlying philosophy, like that of the Epistle to the Hebrews, is of a Platonic cast, which is always congenial to the mystical outlook. The ultimate reality, instead of being, as in Jewish apocalyptic, figured as the last term in the historical series, is conceived as an eternal order of being, of which the phenomenal order in history is the shadow or symbol."[4] Bultmann has concluded that John has completely given up the history-of-salvation perspective in favor of a Gnostic type of outlook. The Johannine Jesus brings the truth, "which is just

---

[3] "Every man" is potential, not actual; see W. F. Howard in *Interpreter's Bible*, VIII, 470.

[4] C. H. Dodd, *The Apostolic Preaching and Its Developments* (1936), p. 157.

the mode of expression of that dualism to which everything earthly is falsehood and seeming."[5] Jesus is portrayed in terms of the Gnostic redeemer myth,[6] of a heavenly divine being who comes from heaven to earth to bring men release from bondage in the world so that they might return to their true home in heaven.[7]

We believe that a careful study of the Fourth Gospel leads to different conclusions. We would in no way minimize the distinctive emphasis and perspective found in John; but it is our thesis that this is a difference of emphasis and not of fundamental theological outlook. The fact is that John does not reflect a genuinely Greek dualism, either Platonic or Gnostic, but a Jewish-Synoptic dualism adapted to a Hellenistic audience. If Christ came from heaven to bring men eternal life, this life does not consist of flight from the world to escape to heaven; it is a life experienced on earth in history that will finally issue in the resurrection. Jesus has come to issue a summons to lost men to hear his voice and to enter into eternal life. And the one whose voice now calls the dead into life will one day be heard by all the dead in the tombs to raise them up unto a resurrection of life or a resurrection of judgment (John 5:25-29). Jesus has come from heaven to bring salvation to the lost, and he will "raise it up at the last day" (6:39). It is God's redemptive purpose that everyone who sees the Son and believes in him may here and now experience eternal life, "and I will raise him up at the last day" (6:39). Jesus is the one sent from heaven to draw a man out of the world unto himself, "and I will raise him up at the last day" (6:44). Jesus has come to give his life

[5] R. Bultmann, *Theology of the New Testament* (1955), II, 11.

[6] *Ibid.*, p. 12.

[7] We cannot here discuss the involved question of the history of this Gnostic redeemer figure. The comparative religions school argues that such a heavenly redeemer must have existed in pre-Christian Gnosticism, even though, admittedly, references to such a heavenly redeemer in pre-Christian literature are completely lacking. More cautious scholars hold that the Gnostic concept of a heavenly redeemer is not pre-Christian but is itself due to Christian influence. See R. McL. Wilson, *The Gnostic Problem* (1958), pp. 106, 225ff.

for men so that he who eats his flesh and drinks his blood may have eternal life, "and I will raise him up in the last day" (6:54).

Here is a reiterated twofold emphasis: God in the person of Jesus visits men on earth that they may in turn look forward to the eschatological resurrection. It is the same basic dualism found in the Synoptic Gospels, even though there is a far greater emphasis upon the present aspect of salvation. The technique of avoiding this twofold tension by excising all eschatological references as later ecclesiastical interpolations is utterly arbitrary and unwarranted.[8] In John, the destiny of the saved is not heaven but the resurrection. John does not conceive of Christ as a heavenly Savior who came from heaven to bring souls lost in the world back to their home in heaven; he came to bring them eternal life on earth—a life that will mean the resurrection of the body at the last day.

This line of thought seems to be contradicted by the saying found in John 14:2-3: "In my Father's house are many rooms; if it were not so, would I have told you that I go to prepare a place for you? And when I go and prepare a place for you, I will come again and take you to myself, that where I am you may be also." It is difficult to deny that these words *can* be interpreted to mean that Jesus will come spiritually upon the death of his disciples to receive their souls and lead them to their eternal home in heaven.[9]

Other scholars interpret the words, "I come again" in verse 3 in the light of 14:18: "I will not leave you desolate; I will come to you" (*erchomai pros humas*), and understand them to refer either to a reunion of Jesus with his disciples after the

---

[8] Bultmann's arbitrary excision of these references has justly suggested the designation "our twentieth-century Marcion" (*Expository Times*, LXVII [1956], p. 98).

[9] See A. M. Hunter, *The Gospel According to St. John* (1965), p. 141. K. Kundsin understands the saying to be a promise that Christ will receive the disciples upon their death by martyrdom, "Die Wiederkunft Jesu in den Abschiedsreden des Johannesevangeliums," ZNTW, XXXIII (1934), p. 213.

resurrection or to the coming of the Holy Spirit.[10] While the promises in 14:18 and 14:28 do have as their context either the coming of the Spirit or reunion after the resurrection, this is not the case with 14:3, "I come again" (*palin erchomai*). The context requires either a spiritual visitation at the death of the disciples, or an eschatological coming.

The idea of a coming of Jesus at death to receive his disciples to himself is found nowhere else in John. Something of this idea may be reflected in Stephen's vision of the Son of Man standing at the right hand of God (Acts 7:59), but it is not Johannine. On the other hand, two clear references to an eschatological coming of Christ are found in the Johannine writings. Speaking of John, Jesus said, "If it is my will that he remain until I come, what is that to you?" (21:22). Dodd speaks of this as a "naive conception of Christ's Second Advent . . . unlike anything else in the Fourth Gospel."[11] This, however, is precisely the point under inquiry, and we believe that 14:3 contains the same promise. Furthermore, in I John, there is even an explicit mention of the Parousia (2:28) and of the appearing of Christ (*ephanerōthē*; 3:2).[12]

This conclusion is strengthened by the fact that in the Gospel the Son of Man is a heavenly being who has descended from heaven to earth (3:13; 6:62) to suffer and die (3:14; 8:28; 12:34), to be glorified (12:23; 13:31), to return to heaven (3:13; 6:62), and to come again in glory (1:51) for the judgment of men (5:27). The saying in 1:51 is most instructive: "You will see heaven opened, and the angels of God ascending and descending upon the Son of Man." Bernard understood

---

[10] See C. H. Dodd, *The Interpretation of the Fourth Gospel* (1953), pp. 395, 404; W. D. Davies, *Invitation to the New Testament* (1966), p. 475.

[11] C. H. Dodd, *op. cit.*, p. 431.

[12] Dodd avoids the force of this evidence by holding that I John and the Gospel do not come from the same hand (C. H. Dodd, "The First Epistle of John and the Fourth Gospel," *Bulletin of the John Rylands Library*, XXI [1937], 129-156; *The Johannine Epistles* [1946], pp. xlvii-lvii). However, this is most unlikely. See W. G. Kümmel, *Introduction to the New Testament* (1965), pp. 310-312.

this to be a promise to Nathanael of the eschatological advent of the Son of Man. Nathanael had voiced faith in Jesus as the "Son of God, the King of Israel," that is, as the political, national Messiah longed for by the Jews, the messianic King who should also be the (messianic) Son of God. Jesus' reply indicates that his messiahship is of another order, involving a higher conception, a more spiritual picture than that of the earthly prince. The same vision is indicated here as that promised to the Sanhedrin (Mark 14:62), with this difference: "The vision that would be the condemnation of the high priest who presumed to condemn Jesus . . . would be the reward of disciples who faithfully accepted Him as the Messiah."[13] More recently, W. F. Howard understands this saying in the same eschatological reference, "The picture we have then is of the heavens opened and angels from above and beneath converging on the Son of Man, the central figure."[14] We conclude that the words "I come again" refer to the Parousia of Christ at the end of the age.[15]

Even if it be granted that John 14:2 is a promise of the Second Coming in the eschatological day, must we not recognize something of a contradiction or an inconsistency between these words and the affirmation about the ample room in the Father's house in heaven where Jesus is going to prepare a place for them? Do these words not assert clearly that the believer's home is in his Father's house in heaven? Is this not analogous

---

[13] J. H. Bernard, *The Gospel According to St. John* (1929) I, 113.

[14] W. F. Howard, *The Interpreter's Bible*, VIII, 490. See also *Christianity According to St. John* (1946), pp. 111f.; A. Corell, *Consummatum Est* (1958), pp. 103f.

[15] See W. F. Howard, *The Interpreter's Bible*, VIII, 700; Wm. Barclay, *The Gospel of John* (1955), II, 181; F. Büchsel, *Das Neue Testament Deutsch* (1949), IV, 146; J. Schneider, *TDNT*, II, 673. C. K. Barrett, *The Gospel According to St. John* (1955), p. 381, hesitantly recognized the primary reference of "I come" is to the eschatological advent of Jesus. See also O. Michel, "Unser Ringen um die Eschatologie," *ZTK*, XIII, N.F. (1932), 173; G. Stählin, "Zum Problem der joh. Eschatologie," *ZNTW*, XXXIII (1934), 239ff.; W. G. Kümmel, *Die Eschatologie der Evangelien* (1936), p. 23.

THE JOHANNINE PATTERN: ETERNAL LIFE

to Socrates, who, in the face of death, said, "I have great hopes that when I reach the place to which I am going, I shall there, if anywhere, attain fully to that which has been my chief object in my past life, so that the journey which is now imposed upon me is begun with good hope"?[16] Or to Philo's thought: "So shalt thou be able also to return to thy father's house, and be quiet of that long endless distress which besets thee in a foreign land"?[17]

The background for the Johannine thought is not, however, the Greek dualism of two worlds and the flight of the released soul from bodily bondage to the freedom of the heavenly realm, as in Plato and Philo. The background is the Jewish development of Old Testament thought, that between death and resurrection the soul or spirit is with God awaiting the resurrection. We have seen that in the Old Testament the conviction begins to emerge that death cannot break off the fellowship God has created with his people, but that somehow this fellowship must continue after death. Judaism developed this conviction further. Fourth Ezra pictures the souls of the dead in "chambers" or "treasuries of souls" where they enjoy great quietness, guarded by angels, awaiting the glory of the resurrection when "the earth shall give up those who are asleep in it, and the dust those who dwell silently in it; and the chambers shall give up the souls which have been committed to them."[18] W. D. Davies has called attention to the fact that in some rabbinic reference, *ha olam haba*—"the age to come"—was used not only of the eschatological age to come when the Kingdom of God would be established on the earth; it could also designate the intermediate state of the righteous dead. However, this is not a movement away from the Hebrew toward the Greek dualism,

[16] Plato *Phaedo* 67B, cf. 108C. "The soul that has passed through life in purity and righteousness, finds gods for companions and guides and goes to dwell in its proper dwelling [*eis tēn prepousan oikēsin*]."
[17] Philo *De Somn.* I, 256.
[18] IV Ezra 7:32; 7:95. See note and references in G. H. Box, *The Ezra Apocalypse* (1912), pp. 33f. See also Enoch 39:4; 22:9.

71

for Davies goes on to point out that "the *olam haba* both IS and COMES, and in those passages where there is mentioned resurrection, the *olam haba* which we enter at death finds its consummation in that *olam haba* which follows the resurrection."[19] This is indeed the opposite of the Greek idea of escape from the world to a transcendent heaven; it is the biblical idea of the coming of heaven to earth.

This is true of the Gospel of John. If Jesus is going away to prepare a place for his disciples, it is not for the purpose of readying a home to which his disciples may at death escape from the world; he will come again to them in the eschatological day to welcome them home. If there is a reference here to the intermediate state, it is coupled with the return of Christ, which is an eschatological event. This fact, together with the references to resurrection, places the Fourth Gospel within the structure of eschatological rather than cosmological dualism. "There is never a hint in his Gospel that the Greek idea of immortality, the mere survival of the soul, has replaced the semitic concept of life."[20]

This eschatological dualism finds further support in the nature of eternal life. Eternal life is not the life of a timeless eternity which has broken into time; it is the life of the age to come which will follow the end of this age. *Aiōnios*—"eternal" —can carry different shades of meaning. Plato uses the adjective *aiōnios* to designate the ideal world which God made before he engaged in the creation of the cosmos. Time was created with the cosmos; the ideal world belongs to that which transcends time.[21] However, the setting of the Johannine *zoē aiōnios* is not Greek dualism but Old Testament eschatological dualism. The idea goes back to Daniel 12:2, where the righteous are raised from the dead into eternal life, that is, the life of the age to come. In Jewish eschatology, "eternal life" is used frequently

---

[19] W. D. Davies, *Paul and Rabbinic Judaism* (2nd ed., 1955), p. 316.
[20] R. Schnackenburg, *God's Rule and Kingdom* (1963), p. 280.
[21] *Timaeus* 37D.

to designate life in God's Kingdom, even though this Kingdom is diversely conceived.[22]

The Synoptic Gospels also speak of eternal life; and here, as in Judaism, it is the life of the age to come. When the rich young ruler asked how to inherit eternal life (Mark 10:17), he was thinking of the life of the resurrection, and Jesus answered him in the same terms. This eternal life is the life of the Kingdom of God (10:23), which will be inherited in the age to come (10:30; see also Matt. 25:46). The coming of the Son of Man will effect a separation of men: the wicked will go into eternal punishment and the righteous into eternal life (Matt. 25:46). In several other places in the Synoptics, the simple "life" is used of this eschatological blessing (Matt. 7:14; Mark 9:43, 45). In the Synoptics the idiom "life" and "eternal life" in its redemptive significance is always a future eschatological blessing (Luke 10:25).

In the Fourth Gospel, life still retains its eschatological character. The usual Jewish attitude is reflected in the Jewish expectation of finding eternal life in the Scriptures (John 5:39). It was a commonplace in rabbinic teachings that the study of the Torah would lead to "life in the age to come."[23] When Jesus said that "whoever does not obey the Son shall not see life" (3:36), he was referring to man's ultimate destiny in the age to come. This eschatological character of life is most vividly seen in John 12:25: "He who loves his life loses it, and he who hates his life in this world will keep it for eternal life." The Johannine form of the saying more clearly sets forth the antithetical structure of the two ages than the sayings in the

[22] See En. 5:9; 10:10; 25:6; 37:4; 40:9; 58:3; 62:14; Ps. Sol. 3:12; II Macc. 7:36; Test. Asher 5:2. The simple word "life" is also used of this eschatological blessing. See Ps. Sol. 9:4; 14:6, 7; II Macc. 7:9, 14; IV Ezra 7:13, 21, 48. For other references, see H. L. Strack and Paul Billerbeck, *Kommentar zum Neuen Testament aus Talmud und Midrasch* (1922), I, 464, 808f., 829; G. Dalman, *The Words of Jesus* (1909), pp. 158-162.

[23] See references in C. H. Dodd, *The Interpretation of the Fourth Gospel*, p. 82.

Synoptic Gospels where the similar thought occurs (Mark 8:35; Matt. 10:39; 16:25; Luke 9:24; 17:33). "The Fourth Evangelist alone has given it a form which obviously alludes to the Jewish antithesis of the two ages: he who hates his soul in the *olam haze* will keep it in the *olam haba*; and consequently will possess *hayye ha olam haba*."[24] The one who drinks of the living water will find it to be a source of life in the age to come (4:14). There is also a food that Christ can give which will produce eternal life (6:27). This eternal life is to be experienced at the last day when the righteous will be brought forth "to the resurrection of life" (5:29). This saying is very close to Daniel 12:2. "Eternal life" is the life of the age to come.

While eternal life is eschatological, the central emphasis of the Fourth Gospel is not to show men the way of life in the age to come but to bring them a present experience of this future life. Here is a teaching that is not found in any explicit form in the Synoptics, that the life of the age to come is already imparted to the believer. The purpose of Jesus' mission was to bring men a present experience of the future life (10:10). He came down from heaven to give life to the world (6:33), to satisfy the world's spiritual hunger and thirst (6:35). This life is not a quickening of any innate powers resident in man; it is the imparting of a new life, mediated through Christ. Those who do not "eat his flesh and drink his blood" cannot share life (6:35). This life is mediated both through Jesus' person and his words. His very words are life (6:63), because they come from the Father who has commanded him what to say, and God's commandment is eternal life (12:49-50).

This life is mediated through Jesus and his word because it is resident in his very person (5:26). He is the living bread who gives life (6:51ff.) and the living water (4:10, 14). God is the ultimate source of life; but the Father has allowed the Son life in himself (5:26). Therefore, Jesus could say, "I am the life" (11:25; 14:6).

[24] C. H. Dodd, *op. cit.*, p. 146.

That this life resident in Jesus is nothing less than the life of the age to come is illustrated by the frequent connection between the present reception of life and its future enjoyment. Drinking of the living water that Jesus gives means that one will have within him a fountain of life that will issue in eschatological eternal life (4:14). The one who partakes of the life in Jesus will live forever (6:51). Those who receive eternal life will never perish (10:28).

The future dimension of eternal life includes the resurrection of the body; and those to whom Jesus has given eternal life, he will raise up in the last day (6:40, 54). Jesus is both life and resurrection. The one who believes in him may die physically; but he will live again in the last day. Since he already has this life through faith in Jesus, he will never die (11:25-26).

These two dimensions of life—present and future—are inseparably associated in Jesus' discourse about his relationship to the Father. Since God is the source of life, it is he alone who can raise the dead, but he has entrusted this prerogative to his Son (5:21). This mission of raising the dead is fulfilled in two stages. The hour has already come when the dead hear the voice of the Son of God and come to life (5:25). That this refers to "spiritual" resurrection, i.e., the present experience of eternal life, is proved by the words, "The hour is coming, and *now* is." This event of rising into life is taking place in Jesus' ministry because the Father "has granted the Son also to have life in himself" (5:26). However, this present experience of life is not all that life means: "the hour is coming when all who a·e *in the* tombs [i.e., the physically dead] will hear his voice and come forth . . . to the resurrection of life, and . . . to the resurrection of judgment" (5:28, 29).

This inseparable relationship between eternal life present and eternal life future places an intolerable strain upon the interpretation that sees the center of the Johannine concept of life as being analogous to Greek ideas of a Platonic eternal life belonging to a timeless realm, which John has then superimposed upon a basic Jewish structure. This interpretation juxtaposes two diverse concepts of life—one Greek and one Hebrew—without establishing an inner bond of essential relationship; and this in turn neglects the data cited above that hold together the present and future aspects of eternal life. Much more satisfactory is Piper's analysis—that John's message of life is rooted in the Old Testament idea that God, who is life, has imparted his life to men through the incarnation of the eternal "word of life," and that the eschatological resurrection is not extraneous to the center of John's thought but is the full manifestation of life in believers.[25]

This can be illustrated by the analogy between the Johannine teaching of life and the Synoptic teaching of the Kingdom of God. It is noteworthy that in John eternal life is first mentioned after the only references in the Gospel to the Kingdom of God (3:35).[26] Both in the Synoptics and in John, eternal life is the life of the eschatological age to come. In the Synoptics, this life is also the life of the Kingdom of God, which belongs to the age to come. However, the unique element in Jesus' preaching of the Kingdom in the Synoptics is that the eschatological Kingdom has invaded this age. The Kingdom has come (Matt. 12:28) while the age to come remains future. In the same way John sees that the life that belongs to the age to come has come to men in the old age. "In this, zoē aiōnios in John resembles kingdom of God in the synoptic gospels. That which is properly a future blessing becomes a present fact in virtue of the future in Christ."[27] Therefore while the idiom is different, and we are not to identify the Kingdom of God and eternal life, the underlying theological structure is the same, though expressed in different categories. If eternal life is indeed the life of the eschatological Kingdom of God, and if the Kingdom is present, it follows that we might expect the Kingdom to bring to men a foretaste of the life of the future age.

We find further support for our thesis in an important Johan-

---

[25] O. Piper, "Life," *IDB*, III, 128f.
[26] C. K. Barrett, *The Gospel According to St. John* (1955), p. 179.
[27] *Loc. cit.*

nine concept that Dodd understands in a thoroughly Greek way: the concept of truth and of genuineness or reality (*alēthinos*). Jesus came into the world to bear witness to the truth (18:37). "You shall know the truth and the truth shall make you free" (8:32). After Jesus' departure, the Holy Spirit is promised, who will lead the disciples into all truth (16:13). It is easy to understand such sayings in the light of the Greek sense of truth as correspondence to reality. Jesus brought to men the pure and eternal reality, as distinct from the world of transient phenomena.[28] The knowledge of that which is truly real sets men free. Truth is reality—the eternal reality of God, manifested in time among men in history to bring them into relation with the timeless world of ultimate reality.

This understanding seeks further support in the idea of genuineness: *alēthinos*, reality versus all unreality. Jesus is the genuine light over against all false, unreal lights (1:9). He is the real bread in contrast to all pretense or seeming (6:32). He is the real vine (15:1); God is the genuine God against all false gods (17:3).

The Johannine concept of truth is susceptible to a very different interpretation, the key to which is suggested in the first two uses of the word in the first chapter. "The Word became flesh and dwelt among us, full of grace and truth" (1:14). "For the law was given through Moses; grace and truth came through Jesus Christ" (1:12). Grace and truth in these verses stand for the Old Testament *chesed* and *emeth* (Hos. 4:1; 2:20). *Chesed* designates God's covenant love;[29] *emeth* his reliability, loyalty, faithfulness.

Because of its importance in John, this merits thorough exposition. When used of men and things, *emeth* designates their trustworthiness and reliability. A man who acts with *emeth* is one whose conduct can be trusted because he recognizes the ties of family or friendship and acts loyally (Gen. 24:49; 42:16; 47:29; Josh. 2:14). A "truthful" witness (a witness of *emeth*)

---

[28] C. H. Dodd, *op. cit.*, p. 176.
[29] AV usually translates "tender mercy," the RSV "steadfast love."

is one whose word can be trusted because it corresponds to the facts (Prov. 14:25). In such uses, *emeth* is close to the Greek *alētheia,* "reality." Deeds or words or reports of judgments have the character of *emeth*—reliability—because they agree with the facts (Deut. 13:14; 22:20; I Kings 10:6; 22:16; Prov. 12:19; Zech. 8:16). "Seed of *emeth*" (Jer. 2:21) is seed whose quality can be trusted. "A peace of *emeth*" is a trustworthy peace, one that endures (Jer. 14:13). "Justice of *emeth*" is justice that can be trusted, which is genuine justice (Ezek. 18:8).

Emeth finds its most distinctive use in the Old Testament in describing God, or rather, in describing the character of God's acts. *Emeth* does not primarily describe God in himself, but the quality of God's acts in dealing with his people. God can be trusted; he is not arbitrary or capricious. Therefore his people can rely upon him to deal with them with *emeth*—faithfully. *Emeth* is often coupled with *chesed,* which designates God's loyalty in fulfilling his promises and his covenant. God manifested his *chesed* and *emeth* by leading Abraham's servant to find a wife for Isaac (Gen. 24:27), by causing Jacob to prosper in the house of Laban (Gen. 32:10), and most notably by giving the covenant at Sinai (Ex. 34:6) and thereby providing the basis of all of God's dealings with his people.[30] God also shows his *emeth* by punishing the wicked (Ps. 54:5); he is acting "in character." The God of *emeth* (II Chr. 15:3; Jer. 10:10) is not the God who is guardian of some abstract entity called "truth" or one who belongs to the realm of eternal truth as over against the realm of appearance; he is the God who can be trusted, who is able to act, and whose care for his people is sure. To be sure, this leads to the concept of the true God in contrast to false or unreal gods; but he is the true God because he is able to act, because he can visit the earth in both blessing and judgment, and because his acts are trustworthy and reliable. God's people are so to glorify God that his *chesed*

[30] See II Sam. 2:6; Ps. 25:10; 40:10, 11; 57:3; 61:7; 86:15; 89:14; 108:4; 111:7-8; 117:2; 146:6.

and *emeth* will be evident, and the Gentiles will have no occasion to ask in derision, "Where is their God?" (Ps. 115:1-2).

God's *emeth* is also eschatological. The future salvation of restored Israel will mean the disclosure of God's *emeth* promised to Jacob, and the *chesed* promised to Abraham (Mic. 7:18-20). God will dwell among his people and "will be their God in *emeth* and in righteousness" (Zech. 8:8). This perfecting of fellowship between God and his people will be the final disclosure of his *emeth*.

In return for his acts of *emeth*, God seeks a response from men in *emeth*. Men who fear God are called men of *emeth* (Ex. 18:21; Neh. 7:2), that is, men who faithfully respond to God's *emeth*. God always acts with *emeth*, but man often responds with wickedness (Neh. 9:33). Men are called upon to serve God with *emeth* (Josh. 24:14; I Sam. 12:24), to walk in *emeth* (I Kings 2:4; II Chr. 31:20; Ps. 26:3; 86:11; Isa. 38:3). *Emeth* becomes essentially the revealed will of God.

This provides background to understand statements where "truth" or *emeth* stands alone. Hezekiah's desire to see "peace and *emeth*" in his days (II Kings 20:19) refers not merely to "security" (RSV), but to a security that results from the faithfulness of God, who preserves his people. The failure of *emeth* is a situation in which men are not living in accordance with the revealed will of God (Isa. 59:15; Dan. 8:12). When "*chesed* and *emeth* meet" and "*emeth* springs up from the ground" (Ps. 85:10-11), God manifests his salvation, filling the land with glory and giving his people what is good (Ps. 85:9, 12). When Jerusalem becomes a city of truth (Zech. 8:3), it will be the place where God's will is disclosed and which faithfully responds to God's will. It will therefore enjoy God's salvation.

Truth and the knowledge of God are related concepts. The disobedience of Israel means that "there is no *emeth* or *chesed*, and no knowledge of God in the land" (Hos. 4:1). However, the future salvation of Israel is described in the words: "I will betroth you to me in righteousness and in justice, in *chesed*, and in mercy. I will betroth you to me in truth (*emunah*, a cognate) and you shall know the Lord" (Hos. 2:20).

"It is obvious that to John *alētheia* is the O. T. *emeth*."[31] This is clear in the first uses of the word at the beginning of John's Gospel (1:12, 14). "Grace" and "truth" stand for the Old Testament *chesed* and *emeth*, and they place the Johannine interpretation of the incarnate Christ squarely in the stream of Old Testament redemptive history. It is notable that this is the one place in the New Testament where the equivalents of the Old Testament *chesed* and *emeth* appear together. The covenant love (*chesed*) and steadfastness (*emeth*) that God had displayed through the history of Israel have now come to fullness in the incarnation. In fact, this fulfillment of God's redemptive acts in history is now such that it stands in contrast to all that God has done before; for the full understanding of God's grace and truth, which could never be attained in terms of the Mosaic law, is now embodied in Christ.

These two sayings indicate that all of the previous manifestations of God's *chesed* and *emeth* in fact pointed to God's deed in Christ. That the contrast between the law and Christ is not meant to be absolute is shown by such sayings as 5:39, where the Old Testament is not an end in itself but a witness to the truth (5:33) that is in Christ (see also 5:46; 1:45). The point of comparison between the law and Christ is suggested by the words in 1:18, "and from his fullness have we all received, grace upon grace." "It is as the inexhaustible gift of God that the Gospel is contrasted with the Law."[32]

Therefore when Christ said, "I am the truth" (14:6), he means that he is the full revelation and embodiment of the redemptive purpose of God. The coming of Christ is the disclosure of the faithfulness of God to his own character, of his continuing purpose to make his saving will known. Christ's entire mission was to bear witness to this saving truth (18:37). In this context, the "truth" is closely allied with Jesus' king-

---

[31] O. Piper, "Truth," *IDB*, IV, 716.
[32] E. K. Lee, *The Religious Thoughts of St. John* (1950), p. 120.

ship (*basileia*). He is a king; but to Pilate, Jesus said that the source of his redemptive rule was not from the world, and was not to be established by physical force.

Now we can understand the saying that initiated this study of "truth." "To know the truth" (8:32) means to come to know God's saving purpose as it is embodied in Christ; and the freedom promised is freedom from sin (8:34), which could not be accomplished under the old covenant but only by the Son (8:36).

This redemptive understanding of the truth is further illustrated by the adjective *alēthinos*. The Greek word carries the sense of something that is genuine and not counterfeit. The word was used on numerous occasions in the Septuagint to translate *emeth* to mean "trustworthy," "reliable."[33] Zechariah 8:3 is very interesting. When God returns to Zion to dwell in the midst of his people, Jerusalem shall be called *polis he alēthinē*. Such a saying would be difficult for a Greek unfamiliar with Semitic idiom, and the Greek hardly conveys the meaning of the Hebrew text, that Jerusalem will be a city where men have responded to God's revelation of himself and loyally walk in his precepts.

The Johannine use of *alēthinos* sometimes carries something of the Greek meaning of "real," but it is the real because it is the full revelation of God's faithfulness. "The true light" (1:9) does not stand so much in contrast to the false and unreal lights of pagan religions as it does to the partial light that preceded Jesus. John was in a sense a light (5:35), but Christ was the full light. The "true bread" (6:32) is that which satisfies spiritual hunger in contrast to the manna that only sustained bodily life. Christ is the true vine (15:1) because he provides the source of real life for those who abide in *him* in contrast to membership in Israel as the vine in the former dispensation (Jer. 2:21; Ex. 15:1-8; Ps. 80:8-16). The true worshippers (4:33) who are to be created by the new revelation

---

[33] See e.g., Ex. 35:6; II Sam. 7:28; I Kings 10:6; 12:24; Ps. 18:10; 85:15; Prov. 12:19; Jer. 2:21; Dan. 10:1 (Theodotion); Zech. 8:3.

in Christ are contrasted with the Jews who think they must worship in Jerusalem and the Samaritans who worship in Gerizim. This does not mean that their worship was false or unreal; but after the truth has come to men in the person of Jesus, men must now worship in this truth. Henceforth such alone are true worshippers, that is, worshippers whose response is determined by God's revelation of truth. This Hebrew idea expressed in Greek language readily shades off into the idea of real worshippers in contrast to those whose worship is unreal; but the center of emphasis is not the reality or unreality of worship, but the revelation of truth that brings worship to its full reality.

God is the "true God" (17:3) not so much because he stands in contrast with false or unreal gods, but because he is the God who in the mission of Christ is acting consistently with his own being, with the relationship that exists between the Creator and a sinful world,"[34] and with his own redemptive purpose. Thus there is a frequent reiteration of the fact that God is true (3:33; 7:28; 8:26; cf. I John 5:20).

God's truth is not only embodied in Christ but is also manifested in his word, for he speaks truth (8:40, 45) and came to bear witness to the truth (18:37). This truth is not simply the disclosure of what God is; it is the manifestation of God's saving presence in the world. Therefore all that Jesus does and offers is true (7:18; 8:16), i.e., in accordance with his nature and with God's plan.[35] This redeeming purpose is God's work (17:6, 14) and is itself the truth (17:17), which is one with the person of Jesus himself (1:1).

This manifestation of God's truth extends beyond the earthly mission of Jesus. After his departure from his disciples, Jesus will send another Helper (*parakletos*), the Holy Spirit, who is called the "Spirit of truth" (14:17; 15:26; 16:13; cf. I John 4:6; 5:7), because his mission also has to do with the outworking of God's redemptive purpose in the world. His mission will be

---

[34] O. Piper, *op. cit.,* p. 716.
[35] *Loc. cit.*

that of bearing witness to Christ who is the truth (15:26), that is, to direct the attention of men to what God has done in Jesus. He will lead the disciples into all truth (16:13). In its Johannine setting, this does not indicate so much an intellectual apprehension of theological truths as a full personal apprehension of the saving presence of God that has come to men in Jesus.

The "many things" that Jesus has not yet been able to disclose to the disciples (16:12) involve the further explication of the meaning of his person and saving works. The work of the Spirit is Christ-centered: "He will glorify me" by giving a larger understanding of what pertains to Christ (16:14). This mission of the Spirit is also described in the words, "he will declare to you the things that are to come" (16:13). This ought not to be understood primarily in terms of predictions of specific future events but in terms of the future consummation of God's redemptive plan in Christ. If the incarnation means the end term of a long series of redemptive acts in which God has disclosed his *emeth*, there remains yet in the future the consummation of the redemptive work accomplished in Christ. This is also the explication of the truth; and it is the work of the Spirit to lead Jesus' disciples into this truth.

The manifestation of the truth demands a response from men. "He who does the truth comes to the light" (3:21; cf. I John 1:6). This is a thoroughly Hebraic phrase, which in the Old Testament meant to act in a trustworthy manner in terms of the bonds of family relationship and friendship (Gen. 24:49; 47:29; Neh. 9:33). Here, to do the truth means to respond to God's revelation of his truth in Christ in the right way. It is "rightness of speech, of motive, and of action, based upon the historical revelation of God."[36] Another way of describing this response is to receive Christ's word, for "everyone who is of the truth hears my voice" (18:37; cf. 10:3; 16:27). This is

[36] E. Hoskyns and N. Davey, *The Riddle of the New Testament* (1947), p. 29.

83

identical with receiving Christ himself (1:11-12), of being born again (3:3). This means to be indwelt by the Spirit of truth (14:17), and by the truth itself (II John 2). All of this is merely commentary on the saying that initiated this study, "You will know the truth and the truth will make you free" (8:32).

As Jesus has come to bear witness to the truth, he commits to his disciples the same task after his departure (17:18). Jesus had "sanctified himself," that is, dedicated himself to his mission (17:19); and as Jesus sends his disciples into an alien world to continue his witness, he prays that they too may be "sanctified to truth" (17:17, 19). This means that the disciples too are to be dedicated to the truth. As Jesus completely committed himself to the task of accomplishing the redemptive purpose of the true God, so his disciples are to be committed unreservedly to the task of making God's saving acts and his words known in the world.

We have devoted considerable attention to the concept of truth in John to try to establish that rather than requiring a Greek dualism of a heavenly world of reality over against the material world of seeming and unreality, the concept of truth in John tends to place this Gospel squarely in the stream of redemptive history. As Werner Kümmel has said, "John, too, sees man as a *historical* being in the midst of this passing age. His dualism of man-world and God is historical, not natural and timeless."[37] What God has done in history in Jesus Christ is done because God is faithful to himself, and all he has done in the Old Testament finds its fullest exposition in Jesus Christ. Furthermore, the theology of John is a theology of God's invasion of history, not a theology of a flight from history. If there is a greater emphasis upon the dualism of above-below, heaven-earth, it is not because such a vertical dualism is incompatible with the horizontal eschatological dualism of the

[37] W. G. Kümmel, *Man in the New Testament* (1963), p. 80.

Synoptics and has displaced it.[38] Neither is it due to the fact that the primitive Jewish Gospel of the Kingdom of God has at this point suffered Hellenization, for the Kingdom of God is also the Kingdom that has come and that will come from the heavens. It may well be true that the reason for the Johannine emphasis on the vertical dualism rather than the Synoptic eschatological dualism and for his particular choice of language is that he was writing his Gospel to refute gnosticizing ideas that minimized the real historicity of Jesus as the place of the divine redemption. However, if there is a difference of emphasis, the dualism of John remains within the total structure of Jewish eschatological dualism, which awaits the consummation of God's redemptive working in the age to come.

We need again to be reminded that the difference between the Synoptics and John is often oversimplified so that only an eschatological dualism of the two ages is attributed to the Synoptics and only a heaven-earth dualism seen in John. The Synoptics have a spatial as well as a temporal dualism, although it is not strongly emphasized; and John has a temporal as well as a spatial dualism. The Synoptics contrast heaven and earth as well as the present and the future; and in John there is not only an earth-heaven dualism but also a contrast between the present and future. The similarity between the two is most vividly seen when both are contrasted with the Greek dualism: neither the Synoptics nor John know of a flight from this world to God; both relate, with differing emphases, the gospel that the God of heaven has invaded history. For this reason we are unable to agree with those scholars who hold that John has converted the Jewish temporal dualism into a Gnostic spatial dualism.[39] The Kingdom of God that belongs to the age to come has already come to men in history, bringing its blessings in advance of the consummation; and the life of the age to come

---

[38] See R. E. Brown, "The 'Vertical' and the 'Horizontal' View of God's Salvific Action," in *The Gospel According to St. John I-XII* (1966), pp. cxv-cxvi.

[39] See Kümmel, *op. cit.*, p. 75.

has already come to men in history without canceling out the hope of a resurrection of life in the age to come. If the emphasis is decidedly different, the underlying theology is basically the same.

Chapter Four

The Pauline Pattern:
Justification and the Life of the Spirit

The main outlines of Paul's theology are quite clear; but acute difficulties arise when questions are raised about Paul's background before his conversion—whether he was a rabbinic Jew, a diaspora Jew, or a Jew deeply infused with Hellenistic ideas[1]—and about the element of continuity and discontinuity between Jesus and Paul. Jesus preached the coming of the Kingdom of God and what men must do to enter the Kingdom; Paul proclaimed a pre-existent divine being who came to earth to die upon the cross on behalf of lost sinners, who was raised from the dead and exalted at God's right hand as Lord over the world. Salvation results from faith in the perfect redeeming work of Christ and issues in personal fellowship with the exalted Lord. Even when, as in our interpretation, the Kingdom of God is understood to be not only the eschatological visitation of God to inaugurate the age to come but also a present event in the person and mission of Jesus, the message of Jesus and the theology of Paul are certainly on the surface, at least, two different theologies that seem to have very little in common.

Advanced critical scholarship has tended to emphasize the elements of discontinuity between Jesus and Paul. The liberals

[1] See W. D. Davies, *Paul and Rabbinic Judaism* (2nd ed., 1958), pp. 1-16; H. J. Schoeps, *Paul* (1961), pp. 13-50; R. Longenecker, *Paul Apostle of Liberty* (1964), pp. 21-64.

87

saw Jesus as an ethical prophet who taught the Kingdom of God as a set of timeless religious and spiritual values; Paul was a theologian who corrupted the pure piety of Jesus into a speculative system of salvation.[2] Bultmann sees Jesus as an eschatological prophet who must be understood in strictly Jewish terms, who proclaimed the imminent end of the world. Paul, on the other hand, was seen as heir to a Hellenized gospel in which the Jewish apocalyptic hope had been fused with the dying and rising cultic deity of the mystery religions and with the descending and ascending heavenly man of Gnosticism. There is for Bultmann no continuity between the historical Jesus and the Christ of the Pauline kerygma, for the Pauline Christ is not a historical person but an altogether mythological figure who can enjoy no continuity with history. Continuity does exist between Jesus and the kerygma, because in the Christian proclamation it is Jesus, resurrected and exalted, who is proclaimed.[3] Jesus and his message are not part of the Christian message but belong only to the presuppositions of the New Testament message.[4]

As is widely known, the so-called post-Bultmannians have sought continuity between Jesus and Paul by discovering the same basic understanding of existence, or by arguing that the same reality came to verbal expression, that is, faith, in both Jesus and the kerygma.[5]

---

[2] For a history of this problem, see V. P. Furnish, "The Jesus-Paul Debate," *Bulletin of the John Rylands Library*, XLVII (1965), 342-381. See also H. N. Ridderbos, *Paul and Jesus* (1958), pp. 3-20.

[3] R. Bultmann, "The Primitive Christian Kerygma and the Historical Jesus," in *The Historical Jesus and the Kerygmatic Christ*, ed. C. E. Braaten and R. A. Harrisville (1964), p. 18.

[4] R. Bultmann, *Theology of the New Testament* (1951), I, 3.

[5] See the surveys by R. Bultmann, *op. cit.*, pp. 31-38; C. E. Braaten, *New Directions in Theology Today. II. History and Hermeneutics* (1966), pp. 67ff.; H. Anderson, *Jesus and Christian Origins* (1964). There is a full-scale defense of this "post-Bultmannian" interpretation of continuity in E. Jüngel, *Paulus und Jesus* (1962); cf. the review of this by J. M. Robinson, "The New Hermeneutic at Work," *Interpretation*, XVIII (1964), 346-359.

It is our thesis that the basic unity between Paul's theology and the message of Jesus is that both proclaim, although in different ways, the invasion of God into human history for man's salvation. Jesus proclaimed the presence of the eschatological Kingdom of God in his person, words, and deeds. As men responded in faith to the presence of the Kingdom, they were assured entrance into the Kingdom in the day of apocalyptic consummation. Paul has essentially the same message, but with different emphases, which embody a larger understanding of the total meaning of the Christ event. Jesus is indeed a man in whom the powers of the age to come have invaded history, but he is in fact far more: He is the pre-existent one who brought the blessings of heaven to men, not only in his life and teachings, but even more by his death, resurrection, and ascension. If Jesus' proclamation of the Kingdom of God means a divine intervention into history in his person with words and deeds to lead men into the Kingdom of God, this same divine intervention is understood by Paul in terms of incarnation, death, resurrection, and ascension. There is the same understanding of redemptive history; the differences are due primarily to different positions in the unfolding of this history. Jesus proclaims the divine invasion in terms of his earthly life and teaching; Paul in terms of his total person and mission.

Paul reflects the same eschatological dualism as the Synoptic Gospels do. The two-age structure is obvious, although explicit references are not frequent. He can speak of the entire future sweep of human existence as consisting of this age and the age to come (Eph. 1:21).[6] He shares with Judaism the view that this age is evil (Gal. 1:4) and under the influence of evil demonic powers (II Cor. 4:4). This age is in the darkness of sin and ignorance, in rebellion against God, and by its own wisdom cannot find God or come to know God (Eph. 2:2ff.; I Cor. 2:6ff.). The Kingdom of God in Paul is chiefly a future eschatological blessing, an inheritance to be received at the

---

[6] We believe Ephesians to be an authentic Pauline letter.

Parousia of Christ (I Cor. 15:50;[7] II Tim. 4:1, 18). The unrighteous, the immoral, the impure, the idolaters, will not inherit the eschatological Kingdom of Christ and of God (I Cor. 6:9; Eph. 5:5).

Eternal life in Paul, as in John, is an eschatological blessing, to be bestowed on the righteous, and stands in contrast to the eschatological wrath of God (Rom. 2:5-8). Eternal life is the final eschatological goal of the entire redemptive process (Rom. 6:22; Tit. 3:7). This goal remains in Paul's thought within the framework of an apocalyptic manifestation of Christ (Col. 3:4; Phil. 3:20). The goal of redemption will include not only individual destiny but also the entire created order. The creation itself will be set free from its bondage to decay and obtain the glorious liberty of the children of God (Rom. 8:21). Although Paul does not use the idiom of the new heaven and new earth, it is the same theology of a redeemed and transformed creation.[8] The goal of redemption involving the entirety of the created order will be accomplished by a transforming theophany of divine glory in the return of Christ; and the destiny of the redeemed will be transformed life in resurrection bodies on a redeemed earth.

It has come to be a commonplace in Pauline studies that even if Paul retains the eschatological perspective, the center of gravity has shifted to "realized eschatology."[9] Cullmann has

[7] On the meaning of this verse, see J. Jeremias in *NTS*, II (1956), 151-159. In the Pastorals, the coming of Christ is designated by *epiphaneia* instead of *parousia*.

[8] See W. Foerster in *TDNT*, III, 1034.

[9] Strictly speaking, the term "realized eschatology" should be used only of C. H. Dodd's view of a *completely* transformed understanding of eschatology in which *"all* that prophecy and apocalypse had asserted of the supernatural messianic community was fulfilled in the Church" (C. H. Dodd, *The Apostolic Preaching* [1936], p. 145). If *all* that Jewish eschatology expected has been experienced by the church in Christ, then there is no further need of any sort of *parousia, apokalypsis,* resurrection, new heavens and new earth. In other words, futuristic eschatology has been translated without remainder into experienced eschatology. However, the term "realized eschatology" has come to be used not only for Dodd's view but also of the view of others who recognize the element of truth in Dodd's construction but who also preserve a real futuristic eschatology.

argued that while the eschatological hope remains as the essential structure of the entire New Testament thought, the work of Christ in history has become the new center of the redemptive time line.[10] C. H. Dodd has gone much further, saying that "by virtue of the death (and resurrection) of Christ the boundary of the two ages is crossed, and those who believe belong no more to the present evil age, but the glorious Age to Come."[11] "They [the death and resurrection] mark the transition from 'this evil Age' to the 'Age to Come.' . . .The day of the Lord has dawned; the Age to Come has begun. The death and resurrection of Christ are the crucial fulfillment of prophecy. By virtue of them believers are already delivered out of this present evil age. The new age is here of which Christ, again by virtue of his death and resurrection, is Lord."[12] It is not an accurate representation of the Pauline thought to say that the boundary here between the two ages is crossed and that we are now already in the glorious age to come, or that the age to come has begun. The age to come remains in Paul an object of hope and of expectation. The present age is evil and remains under the malevolent influence of evil powers (II Cor. 4:4).

Yet Dodd is right in his emphasis that the event in history in Jesus Christ is an eschatological event which in some way is related to the age to come and has significantly changed the structure of the time-line. This is reflected in the fact that while believers continue to live in this age, the death of Christ means deliverance from the power of this evil age (Gal. 1:4). Furthermore, God has brought new transforming powers to renew the minds of believers by virtue of which they need be no longer conformed to this age (Rom. 12:2). Here are two sides of the redemptive event in Christ: the meaning of his death and a new indwelling power which in some real way delivers believers from this age even while they continue to live in it. This can only mean that in Jesus Christ, the powers of the age to come have intervened in this age without having destroyed it, which

[10] O. Cullmann, *Christ and Time* (1950), pp. 81-93.
[11] C. H. Dodd, *op. cit.,* p. 14.
[12] *Ibid.,* pp. 18, 19.

91

is another way of saying that the God who will intervene in the cosmic apocalyptic event at the end of the age has already intervened in Jesus Christ to bring the blessings of the age to come in advance.

It is because of this modification of the redemptive time-line that Paul can speak of the Kingdom of God not only as an eschatological inheritance but also as the realm of present blessing. God has already delivered us from the power of darkness and transferred us *into* the Kingdom of his beloved Son (Col. 1:13). Although he still lives in the old evil age, the believer in some real sense is also already in the Kingdom of Christ. The blessings of this Kingdom are not to be found on the physical level, but include righteousness and peace and joy in the Holy Spirit (Rom. 14:17). Eternal life, which is an eschatological blessing, has come to men in the corruption and decay of the old age. The man in Christ shares the life of Jesus' resurrection and therefore is to walk in newness of life (Rom. 6:4). Men who are dead in trespasses and sins have been raised up out of the grave of spiritual death by faith and have been made alive with Christ (Eph. 2:2ff.).

This can be illustrated by an examination of several prominent Pauline doctrines, particularly those of justification and life in the Spirit—the objective and the subjective aspects of redemption. Furthermore, the eschatological character of both of these events helps to illuminate their relationship to each other. An unfinished debate has been carried on about the center of Pauline theology. Under the influence of the Reformation, many scholars have held that justification was the central substance of the Pauline thought. In recent criticism, a reaction is to be observed against the centrality of justification. Wrede insisted that the whole of Pauline religion could be expounded without mentioning justification, unless it be in the discussion of the law.[13] Schweitzer, who rediscovered the importance of eschatology for Paul, felt that to take justification by faith as a

[13] W. Wrede, *Paul* (1902), p. 123.

starting point would lead to a misunderstanding of Paul, and that this doctrine was only a "subsidiary crater" formed within the rim of the main crater—the mystical doctrine of redemption through being-in-Christ, conceived in quasi-physical terms.[14] Andrews follows Sabatier in describing justification as a "judicial and inferior notion," which makes it difficult to rise to the higher and finer idea of a righteousness which is imparted.[15] Stewart does not downgrade justification as radically as this, but he finds the real clue to the understanding of Paul's thought and experience in union with Christ rather than in justification.[16] Davies follows Wrede and Schweitzer in viewing justification as only a convenient polemic against the Judaizers, which belongs to the periphery of Paul's thought. The central truth is found rather in Paul's awareness of the coming of the powers of the new age, the proof of which was the advent of the Spirit.[17]

We quite agree with Davies that the center of Pauline thought is the realization of the coming of the powers of the new age; but this does not mean in any way a minimizing of the truth of justification in favor of mysticism or the life of the Spirit. On the contrary, it means an equal emphasis on the doctrine of justification; for justification is an eschatological event belonging to the end of the age, which, nevertheless, has already taken place in history because of the death of Jesus Christ. The very truth of justification is an element of realized eschatology.

The truth of justification must be understood against the Old Testament doctrine of righteousness, which has an essentially eschatological orientation. God is the righteous lawgiver and judge; and it is only in the divine judgment, when God will render a judicial verdict, that each man's righteousness or unrighteousness will be finally declared. Only God, who as lawgiver has set the norm for human conduct, can determine

[14] A. Schweitzer, *The Mysticism of St. Paul* (1931), p. 225.
[15] Elias Andrews, *The Meaning of Christ for Paul* (1949), p. 65.
[16] J. S. Stewart, *A Man in Christ* (1935).
[17] W. D. Davies, *Paul and Rabbinic Judaism* (1955), p. 222.

93

whether a man has met that norm and is therefore righteous. The issue of judgment will be either a declaration of righteousness which will mean the acquittal from all guilt, or conviction of unrighteousness and subsequent condemnation. The essential meaning of justification, therefore, is forensic and involves acquittal by the righteous judge in the eschatological day of judgment.

This eschatological significance of justification is seen in several uses of the word *dikaioō*. When Paul says, "Who shall bring any charge against God's elect? It is God who justifies; who is to condemn?" (Rom. 8:33, 34), he is looking forward to the final judgment, when God's verdict of acquittal cannot be set aside by anyone who would bring an accusation which might result in condemnation. When we read that it is not the hearers of the law who in God's sight are righteous but only the doers of the law who *will be* justified, we must look forward to a day of judgment when God will issue a verdict upon the conduct of men in terms of obedience or disobedience to the law (Rom. 2:13). The temporal orientation of the words "by one man's obedience many will be made righteous" (Rom. 5:19) is the future judgment when God will pronounce the verdict of righteousness upon the many. The *"hope* of righteousness" for which we wait is the judicial pronouncement of righteousness, that is, of acquittal in the day of judgment. This acquittal is no longer sought by obedience and conformity to a legal code. Such a legal acquittal was insisted on by the Judaizers who would turn the Galatians away from grace to obedience to the law. The Christian hope of righteousness is through the Spirit by faith (Gal. 5:4, 5).[18]

The eschatological setting of justification is seen even more clearly in one of the sayings of our Lord: "I tell you, on the day of judgment, men will render account for every careless word they utter; for by your words you will be justified, and by your words you will be condemned" (Matt. 12:36, 37).

[18] Cf. G. Schrenk, in *TDNT*, II, 191, 207, 215, 217.

In the eschatological understanding of justification, as well as in its forensic aspect, the Pauline doctrine agrees with that of contemporary Jewish thought. However, there are several points at which the Pauline teaching is radically different from the Jewish concept; and one of the essential differences is that the future eschatological justification has *already taken place.* "Since therefore we have now been justified by his blood, much more shall we be saved by him from the wrath of God" (Rom. 5:9). "Since we have been justified by faith, we have peace with God" (Rom. 5:1). "You were justified in the name of the Lord Jesus Christ" (I Cor. 6:11). In these instances the verb is in the aorist tense, expressing an act that has been accomplished. Through faith in Christ, on the ground of his shed blood, men have already been justified, acquitted of the guilt of sin, and therefore are delivered from condemnation.

Here again we find a further illustration of the modification of the antithetical eschatological structure of biblical thought. The justification that primarily means acquittal at the final judgment has already taken place in the present. The eschatological judgment is no longer alone future; it has become a verdict in history. Justification that belongs to the age to come and issues in the future salvation has become a present reality inasmuch as the age to come has reached back into the present evil age to bring its soteric blessings to men. An essential element in the salvation of the future age is the divine acquittal and the pronouncement of righteousness; this acquittal, justification, which consists of the divine absolution of sin, has already been effected by the death of Christ and may be received by faith here and now. The future judgment has thus become essentially a present experience. God in Christ has acquitted the believer; therefore he is certain of deliverance from the wrath of God (Rom. 5:9), and he no longer stands under condemnation (Rom. 8:1).

Not only is justification an eschatological truth that has been contemporized by the new structure of the ages; the life of the Spirit is also an element of realized eschatology.

95

The Pauline doctrine of life in the Spirit is inseparable from the resurrection of Jesus Christ, for the Spirit imparted to believers is none other than the Spirit of Jesus Christ, that is, the means by which the resurrected and glorified Christ is present with his people. Paul clearly distinguishes between the person of the exalted Christ and the Spirit, and yet there is a close identity in function. In the Old Testament, the *ruach Yahweh* is only infrequently personified as though it were some sort of separate entity (see Isa. 31:3; 40:13; 63:10; Ps. 139:7); usually the Spirit of God is simply God himself or his creative power at work in the world and among men.[19] In the New Testament, the Spirit is both differentiated from God (II Cor. 13:14) and identified with him.[20]

The relationship between the exalted Christ and the Spirit can perhaps be best approached by trying to understand Paul's doctrine of the resurrected and exalted Christ. One basic fact is very clear: the resurrection of Christ did not mean for Paul a return to physical,[21] that is, to flesh and blood, earthly existence. He flatly states that flesh and blood cannot inherit the eschatological Kingdom, not because it is evil, but because it is perishable and of itself cannot transcend the realm of the perishable (I Cor. 15:48-50). The resurrection of Christ is an eschatological event that belongs to the end of this age of sin and mortality and will introduce the righteous into the consummated Kingdom of God in the age to come. Resurrection was not an event that the Jews ever expected to take place in history; it was one of the complex of events that would end history and inaugurate the world to come. Indeed, resurrected

---

[19] See Ed. Schweizer, *Spirit of God* (*Bible Key Words*, 1960), pp. 5-6.

[20] See I Cor. 12:4-6 where the Spirit, the Lord and God were differentiated and at the same time treated as one in their working.

[21] The reader should note that the author distinguishes between the words "physical" and "bodily," as some scholars refuse to do. "Body" is the larger term; "physical" designates a particular kind of body—the fleshly, weak, mortal bodies of present human existence. The opposite of "physical body" is not "spirit" but "spiritual *body*."

life is itself the life of the world to come (Dan. 12:2; Luke 20:35-36).

Paul makes it clear that he regards the resurrection of Jesus as the beginning of this eschatological resurrection. The resurrection, previously viewed as a single event at the end of the age, is now seen to occur in several stages: Christ's resurrection is the "firstfruits" or the first stage of the eschatological harvest; the second stage will take place at the Parousia when those who belong to Christ are raised up; possibly there is a third stage at the *telos* or final consummation at the end of Christ's reign, which will extend beyond the Parousia[22] (I Cor. 15:20-24). In any case, the resurrection of Christ, like the Kingdom of God, is an eschatological event that has taken place in the midst of history. The eschatological nature of Christ's resurrection is another of the crucial redemptive events that require us to see a realized eschatology, a restructuring of the redemptive time-line in Paul. This is why the resurrection means the appearance of life and immortality in the midst of history (II Tim. 1:10).[23]

When we ask about Paul's understanding of the nature of the resurrection of Christ, we encounter mystery. The resurrection was such that Jesus could appear to people in the flesh, even to as many as five hundred at once (I Cor. 15:4-8). Paul appeals to these eyewitnesses of the resurrected Jesus[24] to establish the reality of this event.[25] The argument he develops in I Corinthians is that the resurrection will see a return to *bodily* life but in a form so different that he can only describe it by contrasts

[22] See O. Cullmann, in *The Early Church* (1956), A. J. B. Higgins, ed., pp. 111-112. See also H. St. J. Thackeray, *The Relation of St. Paul to Contemporary Jewish Thought* (1910), pp. 120ff.; W. D. Davies, *Paul and Rabbinic Judaism* (1955), pp. 293ff.

[23] See the author's essay on the resurrection of Christ in *Christian Faith and Modern Theology,* ed. C. F. H. Henry (1964), pp. 261-284.

[24] Note that they are not witnesses of the resurrection but of the resurrected Jesus.

[25] To reject the force of this appeal in the way Bultmann does is a very arbitrary and unwarranted procedure (*Theology of the New Testament,* I, 295ff.).

with the present physical body: perishable-imperishable; dishonor-glory; weakness-power (I Cor. 15:42-44). He says nothing about the constitution or substance of the body, except that it will be a body. It is tempting to interpret his final adjective, *pneumatikon sōma*, in some sort of Stoic sense and understand *pneuma* to mean the substance of which the resurrection body will be formed. The Stoics conceived of *pneuma* as a fine, invisible material substance permeating all things, both animate and inanimate.[26] However, the context renders this interpretation very difficult. The body of this life, a *psychikon sōma*, which balances the future *pneumatikon sōma*, cannot be a body made of *psychē*, for *psychē* is never thought of as a material substance, but primarily as the life of the body, and secondarily as the essential self capable of existing apart from the body. We must agree with Stacey, "two bodies are thus clearly contrasted. One is made of flesh and blood, embodies the *psychē*, and passes away. The other is a supernatural creation, embodies the *pneuma* and lives forever."[27] Paul says *nothing* about the substance or material of the body; he only insists that it will be a body, "wholly possessed by and wholly an instrument of the Holy Spirit, fully adapted to the resurrection life of Christ."[28]

Thus, while Jesus in his resurrection had a real body that could be seen by mortal men, it was a body that belonged to a different order of existence—the realm of *pneuma*. Our problem is that Paul nowhere describes or defines what this means; he merely affirms it. "The first man Adam became a living being; the last Adam became a life-giving Spirit" (I Cor. 15:45). Christ by his resurrection entered the heavenly realm of *pneuma*, and became himself the agent in imparting life to men—a soteriological function elsewhere ascribed to God (Rom. 4:17; 8:11). Yet as the life-giving Spirit, the glorified

[26] E. D. Burton, *Spirit, Soul and Flesh* (1918), pp. 139-140. W. D. Davies, *op. cit.*, pp. 182ff., shows that rabbinic thought sometimes conceived of the Spirit in material terms.

[27] *The Pauline View of Man* (1956), p. 150.

[28] G. W. H. Lampe in *Interpreter's Dictionary of the Bible*, IV, 434ff. See also Ed. Schweizer, *Spirit of God* (1960), p. 63.

Christ works through the Holy Spirit so that functionally Christ and the Spirit can be identified (II Cor. 3:17). Thus Paul can speak of the indwelling of Christ and the indwelling of the Spirit as though they were interchangeable concepts (Rom. 8:9, 10); and of being in the Spirit and in Christ (Rom. 8:9, 10) without any difference of meaning.

This somewhat involved discussion helps us to understand the eschatological structure of Paul's thought. He thinks of two worlds or two spheres of reality: the world of flesh and blood and the world of the Spirit, the world of men and that of God, the realm of creation and that of heaven. However, the realm of flesh and blood is not itself sinful because it is the sphere of the material, nor does man's salvation consist in escape from this world to the heavenly realm. Redemption is not the salvation of the soul but of the total man, including the redemption of the body (Rom. 8:23), and the transformation of the entire creation (Rom. 8:21).

There are times, to be sure, when Paul sounds almost like a Platonic dualist. "For this slight momentary affliction is preparing us for an eternal weight of glory beyond all comparison, because we look not at the things that are seen but to the things that are unseen; for the things that are seen are transient, but the things that are unseen are eternal" (II Cor. 4:17-18). While Paul's expression is indeed analogous to the Platonic dualism of the eternal realm of being versus the temporal realm of becoming, the setting is nevertheless that of eschatological dualism. There is a realm of reality, God's world, heaven, which does not change, whereas the visible realm is one of flux and change. However, it is not therefore evil, even though it is under the burden of sin. The key to the structure of Paul's thought in this passage is the single word "glory," which designates the divine splendor, the visible divine radiance. When God visited men, he displayed to them his glory (*kabodh*).[29] The final eschatological visitation is described as a manifestation of the divine glory. "The earth will be filled with the knowledge of

---

[29] Num. 14:22; Ex. 24:16f.; 33:18; I Kings 8:11.

99

the glory of the Lord as the waters cover the sea" (Hab. 2:14).[30]

Paul sees the revelation of the glory of God as occurring in two events. In the person of Jesus Christ, the glory of the Lord has been revealed to men. "And we all, with unveiled face, beholding the glory of the Lord, are being changed into his likeness from one degree of glory to another" (II Cor. 3:18). Yet this revelation of the glory of God in Jesus Christ is not an open public thing. It is unseen by many who have been blinded by unbelief so that they cannot see the glory of God. Only in the case of believers has "God shined in our hearts to give the light of the knowledge of the glory of God in the face of Christ" (II Cor. 4:6).

However, the same glory that has shined in Jesus Christ is destined to burst forth on all the world in a final eschatological theophany. God's glory is yet to be revealed (Rom. 8:18) at the manifestation of Jesus Christ when the saints will share his glory (Col. 3:4). Believers have in Christ the hope of glory (Col. 1:27) when they will be glorified with their Lord (Rom. 8:17). This is the meaning of the "eternal weight of glory" in II Corinthians 4:17; it is a thoroughgoing eschatological concept.[31] The heavenly glory of God, which will finally be manifested in cosmic-transforming power, has already come to men in history in a veiled form in Jesus Christ, seen only by believers. The eternal world of unseen realities is God's world which will come to earth and thereby transform both man and his world.

The eschatological structure of Paul's thought is seen further in the fact that the very gift of the indwelling Holy Spirit is an eschatological concept. The prophets looked forward to the perfect establishment of God's reign when the enemies of God and of God's people would be either converted or destroyed, the burden of evil upon the natural world lifted so that joy and blessing alone prevail, and God's people, repentant, converted, and obedient be gathered in the redeemed land. The means of

[30] See also Isa. 35:2; 60:1-3; 40:5; 66:18; Ezek. 39:21; 43:2-5.
[31] See G. Kittel, *TDNT*, II, 250.

this conversion is variously described, but one important aspect of this hope was the gift of the Spirit to indwell God's people. The implanting of the *ruach Yahweh* will mean a new heart—a heart of flesh instead of a heart of stone, a life of obedience to God instead of disobedience, and the final realization of the goal of the covenant: "You shall be my people, and I will be your God" (Ezek. 36:28; cf. Gen. 17:7; Ex. 6:7; II Sam. 7:24, *passim*). Jeremiah, viewing the same day of redemption, describes it in terms of a new covenant when God will write his law upon the hearts of his people with the result that all shall know the Lord (Jer. 31:31ff.). Joel sees an outpouring of the Spirit upon *all* flesh—i.e., not only upon judges, priests, kings and prophets, but upon even the least of God's people (Joel 2:28ff.). The important fact to note is that these promises of the gift of the Spirit regenerating God's people are strictly eschatological and belong to the Day of the Lord (Joel 2:31).

Paul recognizes that the gift of the Spirit is an eschatological gift and that the life imparted by the indwelling Spirit is essentially the life of the age to come. This is attested by two Pauline metaphors. The indwelling Spirit is an *arrabōn* and an *aparchē*. The first term is a word used in commercial transactions in vernacular Greek of the earnest-money, or down payment given in advance of the total sum to be paid in full later.[32] The present gift of the Spirit brings a partial but real experience of the life of the age to come (II Cor. 1:22). In the age to come, the acquisition of the full inheritance (Eph. 1:14) will include the redemption of the body. Paul longs to put on the body not made with hands that what is mortal may be swallowed up in life (II Cor. 5:4). Then he will receive a "spiritual body" (I Cor. 15:44), i.e., a body transformed by the Spirit and thereby made imperishable, glorious, and powerful, conformed to the body of Christ's glory (Phil. 3:21). Then alone will the believer know the fullness of life. However, for this Paul must await the resurrection at the Parousia of Christ and the age to

[32] J. H. Moulton and G. Milligan, *The Vocabulary of the Greek New Testament* (1930), p. 79.

come. Meanwhile, the Christian life is far more than hope; it involves more than a "guarantee" of a future experience of life, as the RSV translates it. Christian experience is the life of of the Spirit, which is an initial installment of the fullness of the future life, the same in kind although limited in degree. "Realized" eschatology does not displace realistic eschatology; rather, it is the reality of the life of the age to come which makes possible a partial experience of that life in the present age.

The same thought of eschatological experience is expressed by the word *aparchē*. Properly speaking, this means a gift of firstfruits offered to God, but it is used by Paul of God's gift to man. The life of the Spirit does not exhaust the fullness of God's redemptive gifts, for we still endure the bondage to decay which afflicts all creation. God did not create men that they might suffer and succumb to corruption and death. We are waiting eagerly for the adoption, namely, the redemption of the body. This blessing belongs to the age to come. However, in spite of the fact that we are in this age in bondage to decay and death, we do have the Spirit as the firstfruits of the life of the age to come. Firstfruits means more than the promise given by the sprouting of leaves or the bursting of blossoms; it is more than the expectation held forth by green but indigestible fruits; firstfruits is the actual beginning of the harvest, yet not identical with the harvest itself. Such is the life of the Spirit: the life of the age to come, the beginning of the eschatological harvest, yet not the fullness of that harvest. This life has through the Spirit been made available to human experience even in the midst of the decay and death of this evil age.

Some scholars have seen a distinct Hellenizing of Paul's thought in his developing concept of the intermediate state. To appreciate the problem, we must briefly outline Paul's view of man. One of the finest modern studies of Paul's view of man is found in Bultmann's *Theology of the New Testament*.[33]

---

[33] I, 190-227. See also W. G. Kümmel, *Man in the New Testament* (1963); W. D. Stacey, *The Pauline View of Man* (1950).

Whether one agrees with the details of Bultmann's analysis or not, he has made it clear that such terms as body, soul, and spirit are not different parts of man as in Greek dualism, but are simply various ways of viewing man as a total entity. In this, Paul agrees with the Hebrew view of man against the Greek. *Sōma*—"body"—is not a prison or a shell or a husk; it is man himself. It is un-Pauline to say that I *am* a soul or spirit living in a body, or that I am a spirit and I have a body; I *am* body as well as soul or spirit. This is why for Paul the destiny of man requires the resurrection of the body, for human existence by definition is bodily existence. This completely differentiates Paul's anthropology from Greek dualism. The sanctified Christian life is not one of ascetic denial of the body or of a spiritual transcendence of physical appetites or desires;[34] it is rather a consecration of the body to God (Rom. 12:1; I Thess. 5:24), for the body is indwelt by the Holy Spirit and has become a temple of God and a member of Christ (I Cor. 6:15, 19).

For Paul, the *psychē* or soul is not man's true self temporarily indwelling a house in a foreign land as in Greek thought. *Psychē*, as in the Old Testament, designates the life of the body or man as a living being, a person—the self as alive and active. Man as *pneuma* is man as a willing, self-conscious being. There is another aspect of *pneuma* that Bultmann does not emphasize: man as *pneuma* is viewed in his relationship—potential or real— to God, who is also *pneuma*.[35] However, one thing is clear: Paul never uses either *psychē* or *pneuma* in contrast to the body to designate man's true self which is capable of a blessed existence after the death of the body. Redeemed existence always includes the resurrection of the body at the last day.

There is one passage where Paul seems to entertain a different view. In II Corinthians 5:1ff., Paul says, "If the earthly

[34] We cannot here discuss Paul's doctrine of *sarx*, which, while it involves the body, does not invalidate the interpretation of the body here set forth.

[35] It is impossible here to defend this view. See W. D. Stacey, *op. cit.*, p. 137.

tent we live in [the present body] is destroyed [in death], we have a building from God, a house not made with hands, eternal in the heavens. Here indeed we groan, and long to put on our heavenly dwelling, so that by putting it on we may not be naked. For while we are in this tent, we sigh with anxiety, not that we would be unclothed, but that we may be further clothed, so that what is mortal may be swallowed up by life."

It is not at once clear whether the building from God, eternal in the heavens, refers to the resurrection body to be received at the Parousia, in accordance with Paul's usual thought, or whether it reflects a new development in Paul's thought so that he now believes that there is a glorious body awaiting those in Christ at death which they will wear in heaven (see v. 8) while they await redemption of the body at the eschatological resurrection. The traditional view in the English-speaking world has been the former, namely, that Paul regards the intermediate state as a time of "nakedness," that is, of the existence of the soul or spirit with God while awaiting the resurrection. Paul shrinks from this condition because he believes that full human existence means bodily existence and he instinctively recoils from the idea of being a disembodied spirit. What he longs for is the resurrection body when mortality is swallowed up by life. However, even though "nakedness" is not desirable, and even though he has no revelation from the Lord that the intermediate state is anything but nakedness, he consoles himself by the realization that in spite of its unsatisfactory mode of existence, he will be at home with the Lord (v. 8), and therefore it will be all right.

A number of scholars have defended the other position, that the heavenly house is to be put on at death and that it describes the mode of existence in heaven during the intermediate state.[36] Most of the scholars defending this view see it as a Hellenizing

---

[36] See R. F. Hettlinger in *SJTh*, X (1957), 174-194 both for references and for the argument. This view is supported also by F. F. Bruce in *Peake's Commentary on the Bible,* ed. M. Black and H. H. Rowley (1962), col. 806e.

of Paul's basically Jewish eschatology.[37] Knox thinks that Paul has exchanged the apocalyptic idea of resurrection of the dead for the Greek idea of the ascent of the soul to its true home in heaven. Life in the flesh is exile from the true heavenly home; death means the return from exile to the homeland. However, Paul was not Hellenized enough to think of the flight of the naked soul to heaven; his Jewish background requires him to believe in a heavenly body.[38]

It must be admitted that in this passage Paul does think of two spheres of existence: corporeal existence on earth and life in a sphere beyond, invisible to the eye, with God. To be at home in the body is to be away from the Lord; and to be away from the body is to be at home with the Lord (vv. 6, 8).[39] But it is not at all clear that Paul has exchanged the hope of spiritual, personal immortality in heaven for bodily resurrection. In fact, the very context contradicts this, for Paul is sure that "he who raised the Lord Jesus will raise us also with Jesus and bring us with you into his presence" (II Cor. 4:14).[40]

W. D. Davies has accepted the idea that Paul expects a body of glory at death; but he argues that this is not incompatible with Jewish thought, for the rabbis conceived of the age to come as being both already existent in heaven and being manifested at the end of this age.[41] Davies believes that Paul's thought also changed to the extent that the resurrection of the dead now becomes the manifestation of that which already exists but is "hidden" in the eternal order.[42] Hettlinger believes that the

---

[37] See especially W. L. Knox, *St. Paul and the Church of the Gentiles* (1939), pp. 136ff. "The second Epistle [to the Corinthians] is largely devoted to a complete revision of Pauline eschatology in a hellenistic sense" (p. 128).

[38] *Ibid.*, pp. 137ff.

[39] See the article by W. Grundmann, *ekdēmeo, endēmeo, TDNT,* II, 63-64.

[40] Knox admits that the second coming of Christ survives in Phil. 1:6, 10; 2:16; 3:20; Col. 3:4; but this merely shows how little Paul was concerned for consistency (*op. cit.*, p. 142).

[41] W. D. Davies, *Paul and Rabbinic Judaism* (1955), pp. 309ff.

[42] *Ibid.*, p. 318.

heavenly house is received at death, but it is only a temporary dwelling. There still awaits for the believer the day of resurrection at the end of the age when the body will be redeemed.[43]

Davies is quite right that II Corinthians 5 can be interpreted against a Jewish background. Furthermore, there are clear indications that Paul is still thinking in the framework of Jewish eschatological dualism. The phrase "the god of this age" is ample proof of that (II Cor. 4:4). The use of darkness and light in II Corinthians belongs to Jewish eschatological dualism and not Gnosticism or Hermetic thought. The light that has shined in the darkness (II Cor. 4:6) and the question of fellowship between light and darkness (II Cor. 6:14) reflect eschatological thinking.[44] If we accept the witness of II Corinthians 4:14 that Paul still looks for the eschatological resurrection, and also accept Paul's word that the heavenly house in II Corinthians 5 is *eternal* (v. 1) and not a temporary one, we are pushed back to the traditional interpretation according to which Paul believes in the survival of the soul or spirit after death with the Lord, awaiting the resurrection of the body at the last day.

Hettlinger has made a strong point that the difficulty with this view is that is seems to involve Paul in a contradiction. On the one hand, he shrinks from the nakedness of death as something to be abhorred, but goes on to say that he prefers to die because death means to be with the Lord.[45] These are obviously contradictory statements; but is it not precisely the kind of psychologically sound tension that a man could express when caught in the grasp of strong ambivalent feelings? Death is an enemy; disembodiment is to be abhorred. Both as a Jew and a Christian, Paul could say that his longing is the final and complete victory of life over mortality (v. 4) at the resurrection. But meanwhile, if he must die, even if he has no light upon the state of the dead, it will be all right, indeed far better

---

[43] R. F. Hettlinger, *op. cit.*, p. 193.
[44] See G. E. Ladd, "The Place of Apocalyptic in Biblical Religion," *Evangelical Quarterly*, XXX (1958), 75-85.
[45] R. F. Hettlinger, *op. cit.*, p. 177.

(Phil. 1:23), for it means to be with the Lord even without resurrection. It is fellowship with the Lord, not the state of the dead, which Paul desires.

We have here in terms of personal destiny the same tension between earth-heaven and present-future found in the Gospels. This twofold tension is vividly seen in one of Paul's latest writings: Philippians 3:20-21. "But our commonwealth [i.e., our home country] is in heaven, and from it we await a Savior, the Lord Jesus Christ, who will change our lowly body to be like his glorious body, by the power which enables him even to subject all things to himself." In Philippians 1:23, he expresses his desire to "depart and be with Christ, for that is far better." Our homeland—our ultimate destiny—is not this world with its sin, its evil, decay, and death. But if our true home is heaven, this does not mean that the disembodied redeemed soul flies away to heaven there to abide in glory; it means that Christ will come from heaven to earth bringing with him the heavenly life, transforming our lowly mortal bodies of flesh and blood to conform to his glorious body; and this transformation does not occur at death when the soul departs to be with Christ; it occurs at the Day of the Lord when "God will bring with him those who have fallen asleep" (I Thess. 4:14).

The results of this examination of Paul's thought on the intermediate state are consistent with our thesis that Paul never views the final destiny of man to be a flight from the world to God; his hope remains the resurrection and a redeemed order. His theology is to be understood in terms of an eschatological *Heilsgeschichte*: the invasion by God into human history in Jesus Christ to bring to men an advance experience of the eschatological blessings of justification and of the life of the Spirit. But this invasion into history loses its meaning when cut off from the eschatological consummation. The pattern of Paul's thought can be subsumed in the word: he who began a good work in you—and for you—will bring it to completion at the day of Jesus Christ (Phil. 1:6).

Conclusion

We have attempted in the preceding pages to illustrate the elements of unity and diversity in the most important segments of New Testament theology. The Synoptic Gospels, John, and Paul share a common basic theological perspective, which stands in continuity to Old Testament theology in contrast to Greek dualism. Greek thought as illustrated by Plato, Plutarch, and Philo conceived of a cosmic dualism and an analogous anthropological dualism. Man consists of two parts, soul and body, by virtue of which he belongs to two worlds, the noumenal and the phenomenal. The phenomenal world is not *ipso facto* evil, as in later Gnostic thought; but it is hostile and inhibiting to the freedom of the soul. "Salvation" therefore is found in escape from the phenomenal world and flight to the noumenal, which alone is the realm of ultimate reality.

The Hebrew view can be said in a real sense to believe in two worlds: heaven and earth. God dwells in heaven and man on earth. But man's true existence is decreed by God to be on the earth, for man as creature stands in solidity with the total creation. Fullness of life is found in fellowship with the God of heaven, who constantly visits man in his historical existence to bring the blessings of divine favor. Man's salvation is not flight from earth to heaven, but the perfecting of man on earth together with the perfecting and redemption of the world itself.

Thus the basic Hebrew dualism is eschatological; it finds

salvation in a final eschatological visitation of God to redeem and transform his fallen creation. The fullest expression of this hope looks for a new order described as new heavens and a new earth (Isa. 65, 66).

The Synoptic Gospels picture this Old Testament hope in process of fulfillment. In the person and mission of Jesus of Nazareth, the Kingdom of God has come to men in history, bringing to them many of the blessings of God's kingly rule. The God of heaven has visited men on earth to redeem them in fulfillment of the Old Testament hope. The consummation of this hope, however, awaits a second divine visitation in the apocalyptic day. God's visitation in history and in the eschatological day are two aspects of a single salvation promised by the prophets. There is a twofold dualism, much like the prophets. Man on earth is contrasted with God in heaven; but the most basic dualism is eschatological. The new redeemed order is made possible by the invasion of the Kingdom of God into history in Jesus of Nazareth; and it will be realized in the last day in the eschatological coming of the Kingdom.

We have defended the view that the fundamental structure of the Johannine theology is historical and eschatological, even though the emphasis is quite different. John preserves an inescapable if minimal eschatology; all that eternal life means will be realized only in the resurrection at the last day. But John is far more interested in the meaning of the divine invasion for God's people in history—he calls it incarnation (John 1:14). The coming of Jesus Christ from God's world to the earth means that men can experience eternal life—the life of the age to come, even while they live in the world of darkness and death. Although John does not emphasize it, this eternal life is the life of God's Kingdom. Jesus has come to bring to full revelation all that God promised in Moses and the prophets, and men may now enter into the reality promised in the Old Testament. John emphasizes the dualism of God in heaven versus man on earth far more than the Synoptics; but this dualism is one of the invasion into history of God's Son, not one of man's flight from history to find salvation in the heavenly world.

Paul has the same twofold dualism of heaven versus earth and this age versus the age to come. He finds salvation in the coming of Jesus Christ in the flesh to effect in history justification by his cross and the conquest of death by his resurrection. Paul looks back upon an event accomplished in Christ, and enlarges upon its redemptive meaning. It is again a theology of divine invasion, issuing finally in a redeemed order that will include the resurrection of the body and the redemption of all creation. Paul emphasizes in a way that would have seemed strange to the prophets the contrast between the present world of human experience and the world of God. However, he never views this world as *ipso facto* evil; he still regards it as God's creation, and the object of redemption. He has no fundamental dualism of man as soul/spirit versus body/flesh. The things of the body and of this world can indeed impair the life of the redeemed spirit; but they do this by becoming an object of affection and thus competing with God for man's devotion. While Paul's language sometimes is close to that of Greek cosmic dualism, he stands in the theology that finds the ultimate salvation not in flight from this worldly order to the heavenly, but in the redemption and transformation of the earthly and bodily by the heavenly. This will occur in the eschatological disclosure of the heavenly world of God (glory) by which the entire earthly order will be transformed to share the divine glory.

The entire Bible finds its unity in what can best be called holy history—*Heilsgeschichte*. It is a record and interpretation of the events in which God visits men in history to redeem them as persons and also to redeem them in society—in history. This means finally the redemption of history itself.

Diversity occurs because of different stages along the redemption line and the differing ways in which the redemptive event may be interpreted. The prophets see this event from the perspective of promise, with a strong emphasis on the earthly and historical meaning of this divine visitation. The Gospels see it in process of fulfillment in the mission of Jesus. Paul looks back upon an accomplished event, while he still looks upward to the God who has come to men in Christ, and forward to the new world at the consummation of history. The entire Bible is an exposition of the theology of God, who comes to man in history to redeem man and history.